Of tricksters, tyrants and turncoats

Of tricksters, tyrants and turncoats

more unusual stories from South Africa's past

Max du Preez

Published by Zebra Press
an imprint of Random House Struik (Pty) Ltd
Company Reg. No. 1966/003153/07
80 McKenzie Street, Cape Town, 8001
PO Box 1144, Cape Town, 8000, South Africa

www.zebrapress.co.za

First published 2008
Reprinted in 2008

3 5 7 9 10 8 6 4 2

PUBLISHER: Marlene Fryer
MANAGING EDITOR: Robert Plummer
EDITOR: Marléne Burger
PROOFREADER: Lisa Compton
COVER DESIGNER: Doret Ferreira, dotted line design
TEXT DESIGNER: Natascha Adendorff-Olivier
TYPESETTER: Monique van den Berg
INDEXER: Robert Plummer
PRODUCTION MANAGER: Valerie Kömmer

Set in 11 pt on 15 pt Adobe Garamond

Reproduction by Hirt & Carter (Cape) (Pty) Ltd
Printed and bound by Paarl Print, Oosterland Street, Paarl, South Africa

ISBN 978 1 77022 043 0

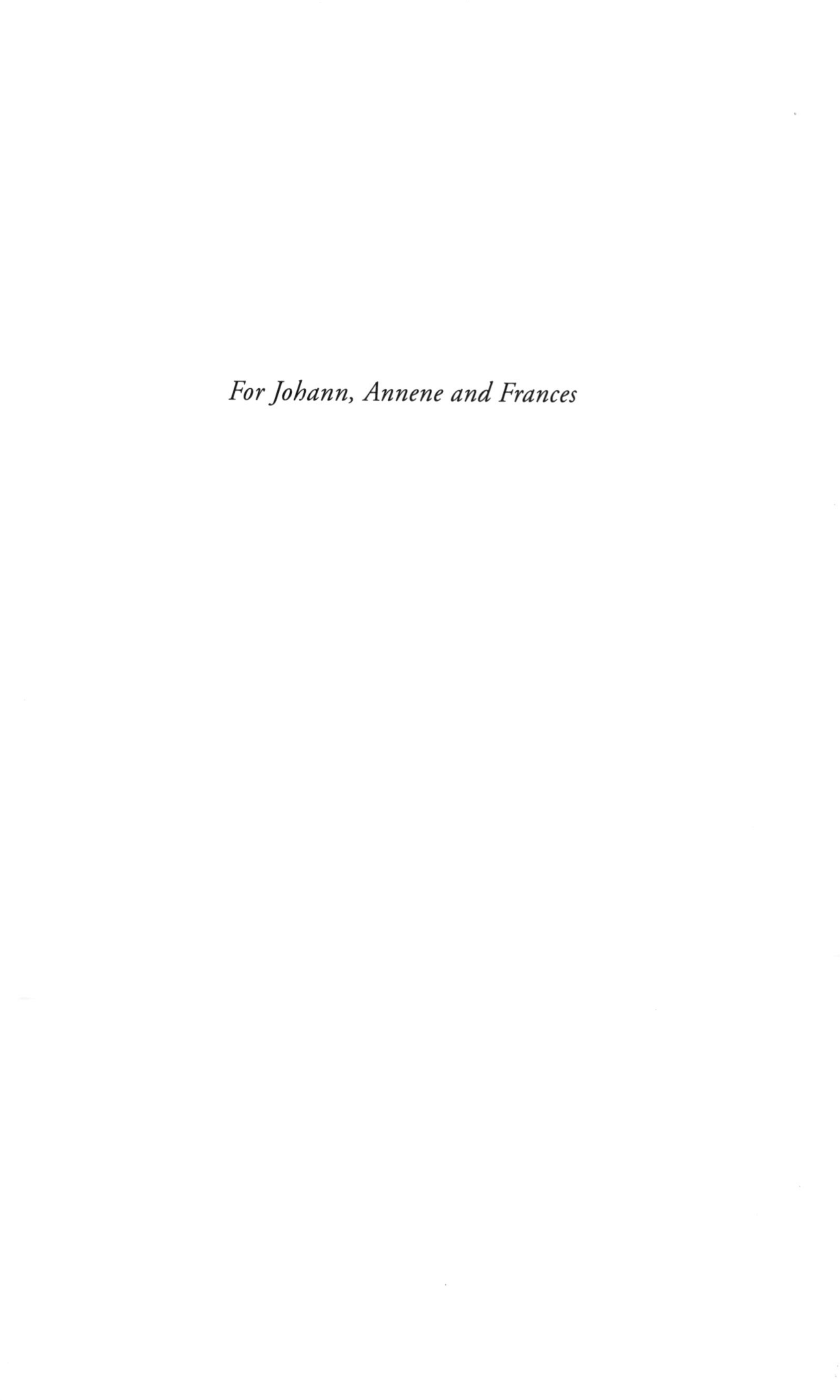

For Johann, Annene and Frances

Contents

Preface

I'M WRITING THIS FROM THE BALCONY OF A SMALL HOTEL in the ancient city of Mostar, Bosnia-Herzegovina. A hundred metres away, I can see the ruins of a once magnificent and very old building, bombed to smithereens in 1993 and not yet restored. The Serbs and the Croats shelled the town from the hills to my left and right and reduced Mostar's Old Town to rubble, including the bridge and the main mosque that were built in the mid-1500s.

Both bridge and mosque are in the Muslim sector, while my hotel is on the edge of the Croat sector. Most of the Serbs who lived here have been driven out. Yesterday, a local community activist told me in graphic detail of the deep resentments still smouldering in the three communities.

She also showed me the history syllabus for the high schools in the three communities of Bosnia. The pupils live in the same towns. They speak the same language. They look exactly the same. And yet they are told that they have almost nothing in common. Their history teachers teach them that the "others", "they", were evil enemies of "us" and never the twain shall meet.

Bosnia and three other regions of the former Yugoslavia I've been to on this trip – Serbia, Kosovo and Croatia – broke my heart. Beautiful, interesting, cultured people, but people with hearts filled with resentment and prejudice. The old saying that one man's war hero is another's war criminal is an absolute reality here. The people have become the victims of their divided history.

I wish someone would ask me to write a Balkan version of my

first book of "unusual stories from South Africa's past", *Of Warriors, Lovers and Prophets.* The people of the former Yugoslavia need to be informed that history can be more than a source of shame, guilt and anger. The Croats and Bosniaks (as Bosnian Muslims are now called) of Mostar should start realising that the stories of their region's past would be better used to unite and bring people closer to one another rather than to hate and divide.

The war in the former Yugoslavia ended more or less at the same time that South Africa's political settlement came into effect in 1994. I've acted a bit like an evangelist on this trip to the Balkans, telling all who might hear how we have been discovering our joint history and heritage, what radical progress towards greater social cohesion we have made during the past fourteen years.

To those who have shown interest in my belief about the role the telling of stories from the past can play, I've given a copy of *Of Warriors, Lovers and Prophets.* Some read the book on the same day and expressed interest in more of the same. Many older people told me it was too late for them – in the words of one, "You can't un-brainwash me any more."

The feedback I received about *Warriors* told me that it wasn't too late for most of us in South Africa. The book had been on the shelves for only six months or so when I realised there was going to be a need for a follow-up. This is it.

I was truly overwhelmed by the response to *Warriors.* I know of two young men who changed their plans and went to study history after reading the book. I met another young man who became a regular reader (and buyer) of books after reading *Warriors* – the first book his mother could ever get him to read.

A woman told me her brother, who had emigrated three years earlier, became so nostalgic and proud when he read *Warriors* that he moved back home.

I was contacted by descendants (and in some cases, wannabe-relatives) of some of the characters in *Warriors,* wanting or giving more information.

I was invited to talk to a number of high school history classes (my apologies to those I couldn't get to) and I have been heartened by the enthusiastic response young people from all backgrounds have shown to stories from our past.

This was all music to my ears. More than ever, I'm convinced of the power of history as storytelling. It is a tool that can be very effective in promoting healing and social cohesion in society.

I also believe that it can be an antidote to the rootlessness and drifting of so many young people. It can help bring those minority groups who feel marginalised back into the mainstream of the nation and give them a sense of belonging.

During my research for this book, as was the case with *Warriors*, I was struck by my emotional reaction to some of the characters in our past. I was deeply moved by the desperation of the Khoi woman Sara, who hanged herself in a sheep shed in 1671. I was intrigued by the Xhosa mystic and war-doctor Makhanda, impressed by the power of the female warrior chief Mantatisi, proud of the Boer War heroine Nonnie de la Rey.

That's the thing about the people of post-liberation South Africa: we can pick our ancestors. Mantatisi is definitely one of mine. I hope my black compatriots who read this book will feel a similar affinity for, say, Nonnie de la Rey, and claim her as their own.

This book follows the same recipe as *Warriors*. There are no wordy footnotes; no pretentious intellectual polemics; no effort to punt any form of academic thesis. I can promise that this book will not bore anyone. At the same time, the research that went into the stories was impeccable and can stand any academic scrutiny. There is no fictionalised dialogue. I made up nothing. And I tried to be as open-minded, even-handed and balanced as I could.

Another characteristic this book shares with *Of Warriors, Lovers and Prophets* is my sensitivity to avoiding any possibility of my storytelling evoking feelings of guilt among certain groups of people. I feel strongly that we should know our history with all its warts,

but that we should be mature enough to say, I will not allow the sins of my forefathers to paralyse me with feelings of guilt and shame.

When someone tries to lay that trip on you, you should feel confident and secure enough to tell him or her where to get off. The men and women who feature in the stories of our past are neither more nor less than human beings, good, evil and in between. Don't allow a single one of them to become a burden of guilt or shame for you, simply because you share some genetic, ethnic or cultural connection with them.

I have said before that I'm no historian. My trade, my gift, is investigative journalism. I've been mixing my craft and my passion for history lately. My journalistic nose sniffs out fascinating characters and stories that historians often miss. Then I put on my reporter cap and follow their trail.

I maintain history is more fun than fiction.

MAX DU PREEZ
MOSTAR
SEPTEMBER 2008

1

Two Women at the Cape

On the morning of 18 December 1671, the body of a young woman was found hanging by her neck from the rafters of a sheep shed in present-day St George's Street, Cape Town.

Her name was Sara. She was a Khoi woman. Suicide was completely unknown in the Khoikhoi culture – she was probably the very first of her people to take her own life.

The sheep shed belonged to a woman named Angela van Bengalen, who came, as her name indicates, from Bengal, an area today shared by India and Bangladesh. She was one of the first emancipated slaves at the Cape, having been declared a "free black" and given a plot of land to farm.

It was Angela van Bengalen who found Sara's body. These are the stories of two unusual women who lived at the Cape in the earliest days of European settlement.

Sara

The Khoikhoi were the descendants of the hunter-gatherers who had lived in Africa since time immemorial. Some two thousand or more years ago, they came in contact with Bantu-speaking cattle farmers in what is known today as Botswana. The new cattle herders quickly spread all over southern Africa, all the way down to the farthest tip of the continent.

When the first European seafarers – sailing with Portuguese

navigator Bartholomew Dias – set foot on southern African soil in 1488, they were met on the beach by Khoikhoi. From 1652, when the Dutch East India Company's Jan van Riebeeck arrived in Table Bay to establish a permanent settlement at the Cape, the Khoikhoi were forced to share their land with the new arrivals.

The Europeans called the cattle herders Hottentots. Some say this was because of the complex click-sounds in their language, while others believe it was because of their typical repetitive dances. The people called themselves Khoikhoi – "men of men" – or, in some dialects, Kwekwena.

The new settlers failed to recognise the fascinating culture, intricate social structures and spirituality of the Khoikhoi and simply regarded them as savages, who on the one hand had to be "uplifted" and, on the other, used as sources of cattle and labour.

So from the first months after arriving at the Cape, the Dutch tried to "tame" some Khoi children, although almost always letting them go after a few weeks or months. They didn't take to the European discipline, customs, lack of freedom and lack of space, it was said.

But sometimes a child did stay, as was the case with a girl called Krotoa, niece of the famous chief of the Goringhaikona or Strandlopers, Autshomato. The settlers called him Herry and employed him as an interpreter and intermediary for years.

Krotoa lived in Van Riebeeck's own household because he believed the assimilation of Khoikhoi into Dutch cultural life was desirable. His wife, Maria de la Quellerie, taught Krotoa to speak Dutch and to be a good Christian girl. She stopped wearing the traditional Khoi *karos*, a cloak made of animal skin, and dressed for the most part in a long skirt and a loose jacket, almost like Indian women.

Krotoa was baptised and given the new name of Eva. By the time she was a teenager, she could speak Dutch fluently as well as some Portuguese, and became the Europeans' most reliable interpreter. The

departure for Batavia in 1662 of the Van Riebeecks – her Dutch "family" – was a setback and she started spending more and more time with visiting sailors.

For a while, Krotoa tried to stay in touch with her own people, but after she married a VOC official, Pieter van Meerhoff, in 1664 and had three children with him, she became completely alienated. (Her daughter, Petronella, married Daniel Zaijman – most Saaymans, Saaimans and Zaaimans in South Africa today are her descendants. My grandmother was a Saayman.) Van Meerhoff was killed four years later while on an expedition to buy slaves in Madagascar.

Krotoa apparently went back to her wayward ways before her marriage. According to an inscription in the governor's Day Register, a year after her husband's death she was reprimanded because she insulted the commander at his table, was drunk in public and "lived a scandalous life". Krotoa's reaction was to leave her children at the fort and go to live rough with some other Khoikhoi among the dunes at Mouille Point.

Krotoa had become an alcoholic. Her children were taken away from her and she was arrested and held for some weeks in a cell before being banished to Robben Island, where she died on 29 July 1674.

Sara was another young Khoi woman who chose life with the Europeans. She was only five years younger than Krotoa and probably also from the Goringhaikona, a clan that owned no cattle and lived at the foot of Table Mountain. Her mother had worked for a white family shortly after 1652.

We don't know what Sara's Khoi name was; Sara was probably the name given to her when she was baptised.

Like Krotoa, Sara spoke both Dutch and Portuguese fluently. There were many Portuguese-speaking slaves at the Cape at the time. Like Krotoa, she wore proper dresses and shoes and lost contact with her Khoikhoi relations. And, like Krotoa, she became a Christian.

One can surely speculate that Sara must have seen Krotoa as a kind of role model, at least early on. Krotoa moved in the high

social circles of the Dutch and then married a senior white civil servant, who must have had quite a bit of money and status.

Sara worked for the bailiff, Hendrik Lacus, and his wife, Lydia de Pape, who was recorded as having been a witness to the baptism of Krotoa and Pieter van Meerhoff's child. In 1667, Lacus was caught stealing company property and sent to Robben Island before being deported in 1670.

Karel Schoeman, the researcher and writer who probably knows the most about the early days of European settlement at the Cape, speculates in *Kinders van die Kompanjie* that Lacus's deportation was probably as disastrous for Sara's fortune as had been Maria de la Quellerie's departure for Krotoa six years earlier. Left vulnerable and alone, Sara could no longer even rely on the support of her own family.

Sara was twenty-four years old when she killed herself on 18 December 1671. The bailiff who wrote the report of her suicide, Hendrik Crudop, recorded that she had been living as the concubine of a Dutch official.

However, the doctor, Willem ten Rhijne, wrote that Sara hanged herself out of "despair" because a white man who wanted to "further his lust" had promised to marry her, then gone back on his word.

Suicide was regarded as something terrible by the Dutch authorities at the time, and in fact had been declared a crime. But it would only have been a crime if committed by a European, because the Dutch had no legal jurisdiction over the Khoikhoi. Crudop's report dwelt at length on proof that Sara had become westernised and part of the white community, which meant she was indeed subject to their laws. Her body had to be dishonoured as if she had been Dutch, because "such as live under our protection are rightly called our subjects".

Crudop used strong condemnatory language in his report to the Council of Justice. He called Sara a "beast" who had been driven by the devil, and recommended that the strongest possible steps be taken.

Why should the death of a mere Khoi servant have stirred up so much emotion among the settler community? It seems they saw Sara's suicide as a rejection of European values and as a blatant act of ingratitude after all the Dutch settlers had done for her.

The Council of Justice agreed with Crudop and ordered that an example be made of Sara's dead body. A hole was dug under the threshold of the shed where she had hanged herself and a mule then dragged her body through it – according to an old European custom, this was done in order not to dishonour the threshold of a building.

The body was taken to the place near the fort where executions took place and put up on a forked post so everybody – settler, Khoi and slave – could see it and be warned. When the post fell over a few weeks later, the order was given for it to be erected again immediately.

Sara's body was left for birds to pick at and eventually to rot. Assimilation into European society didn't work for her.

Angela van Bengalen

In 1657, Dutch East India Company (VOC) commander Jan van Riebeeck bought two female slaves from Pieter Kemp, commander of the *Amersfoort*, who was on his way home from the East. Angela and Domingo van Bengalen were among the very first slaves at the Cape.

Angela (also sometimes referred to as Ansiela) worked in the Van Riebeeck household at the fort and quickly learnt to speak Dutch. Just before he left for Batavia in 1662, Van Riebeeck sold Angela to one of the senior officials at the Cape, Abraham Gabbema. This meant that Angela continued to live at the fort, where senior VOC officials were housed, in what was regarded as a privileged position for a slave.

On 13 April 1666 Gabbema, who was also leaving for Batavia, set Angela van Bengalen and her three children free out of "pure fondness" and because of her good and faithful service to the Gabbemas and their children. Angela was only the third slave at the Cape to be manumitted; the two before her married white men.

Gabbema set one precondition: Angela had to be trained for six months by free burgher Thomas Muller, a baker and member of the Council of Policy. Gabbema felt that without training, she would be too vulnerable as a single young black woman in Cape society. The Mullers, members of the social elite, were good and caring mentors and her time with them served her well. Angela van Bengalen was one of the most fortunate slaves at the Cape.

In February 1667, at her request, Angela was granted a plot in what is today Cape Town's central business district – according to some researchers, on the corner of present-day St George's and Kasteel streets.

She must have been given a garden plot, probably just to the south of where her house was, because there is later reference in company records to transformation of her plot "from a wilderness to a garden with great labour and expense".

Angela was doing so well that she hired a slave named Scipio Africanus in 1668. Like Angela, he was from Bengal. She was one of the very first Cape residents to have the services of a slave.

In the same year, Angela took another step towards integration with the free society at the Cape when she was baptised with another slave, Catharina. A few months later she baptised her son, calling him Pieter.

And then, at the end of 1668, Angela van Bengalen married Arnoldus Willemsz Basson, a former VOC soldier who was a tavern-keeper and fisherman, though he later became a farmer and land-owner. According to official records, Arnoldus bought two slaves from Bengal, Isaac van Bengalen and Antonij van Bengalen. Interestingly, Angela herself also bought two Bengali slaves later in life.

Angela kept the plot that she had been given, and it was here that the tragic Khoi woman, Sara, died in 1671. She must have worked for Angela, because there is no other explanation for her choice of Angela's sheep shed as the place to commit suicide.

Church records reveal that Angela and Arnoldus baptised seven

children between 1670 and 1695. Angela became the matriarch of the Bassons, a prominent Afrikaner family, but she also had three children, probably also fathered by European men, while she was still a slave. One of these was Anna de Koning (her father was obviously a De Koning), who married Oloff Bergh, a Swede who worked for the VOC and was a personal friend of Commander Willem Adriaan van der Stel.

Angela's husband died in 1698. Records show that he owned several plots in Table Valley and a farm in Drakenstein, had five slaves, two hundred and sixty sheep and seventy-three head of cattle. Angela looked after her husband's estate very well and expanded it considerably over the next twenty years.

Her children did equally well. Angela's son Willem held various profitable VOC concessions, while her other sons became wealthy farmers and her daughters married Dutch men. Her son-in-law Oloff Bergh became the head of the garrison and a member of the Council of Policy. Oloff and Anna were members of the Cape's high society.

Angela van Bengalen died in 1720. She still had her house and garden in St George's Street, along with eight slaves – one from Bengal – and owned a farm with three hundred sheep and sixty-three head of cattle. The 6 495 guilders she had inherited from her husband had increased to almost 15 000 guilders.

Her daughter Anna Bergh died in 1733 as the wealthiest woman at the Cape. She owned several houses and plots in Table Valley and had also bought the farm Constantia from Simon van der Stel. It is still one of the most prestigious wine farms in the world. Anna also owned two farms near Piketberg and a house on the Heerengracht, where her twenty-four adult slaves and their children lived.

2

The Unlikely Pageboy

THE EUROPEANS WHO MET WITH THE KHOIKHOI AT the Cape during the seventeenth century believed that these aboriginal people had to become like them in order to be worthy human beings. Apart from the experiments to turn young Khoi women into domesticated little Christian girls in frilly dresses, there were also a few efforts to teach young men the ways and languages of Europe.

I told the story of Coree, the Khoi chief who was taken to England in 1613, in *Of Warriors, Lovers and Prophets*. Sir Thomas Smythe, governor of the English East India Company, took him to London, where he attempted to teach him the English language as well as English culture, and how to dress and eat like an Englishman.

Coree stubbornly refused to cooperate, insisting they take him home. But when he was back at the Cape, it turned out that he had indeed learnt certain things. Instead of becoming a tame agent of the English, he told his people that they were being taken for a ride.

In 1632, the English captain John Hall took Autshomato, leader of the Strandlopers and uncle of Krotoa, on a journey to Bantam in Java. He was taught some English and how to entertain the captain, so that he could act as postmaster and interpreter when British ships dropped anchor in Table Bay.

Autshomato also served as an intelligence gatherer on Robben Island for the English, but he was even more valuable to the Dutch when they set up a refreshment station in 1652. From the moment

they set foot on Cape soil, there was someone who could interpret for them and liaise with other Khoikhoi.

The Dutch also took a Khoi leader overseas to prepare him to be their agent. Nommoa, or Doman, as the Dutch called him, was the third interpreter and intermediary used by the Dutch, following in the footsteps of Autshomato and Krotoa. But what made Doman different from his predecessors was that he did not just try to make a quick buck or suck up to the rich and powerful. Doman was a political animal, and one of the first Khoikhoi resistance leaders.

History professor Richard Elphick, one of the foremost experts on Khoikhoi history, believes Doman's hostility to the Dutch began when they took him to Batavia in 1657 to improve his Dutch and prepare him for his future as an interpreter and intermediary.

"While in Java he was apparently struck by the magnitude of the threat which the Dutch could pose to an indigenous society," Elphick writes in *Khoikhoi and the Founding of White South Africa.* "At the same time he witnessed the climax of the spirited resistance which the Bantamese put up against the Dutch domination of the north shore of the island."

Karel Schoeman agrees. He writes in *Kinders van die Kompanjie* that Doman's stay in Batavia helped him realise that "the authority of the Company and the power of the whites, considerable as it was, could be questioned and opposed; and that with a significant measure of success".

Doman's clever deceit started while he was still in Batavia. To make sure he got home quickly and safely, he told Commissioner Joan Cunaeus that he wanted to become a Christian and that he was so taken with the Dutch that he couldn't even imagine living with the Khoikhoi again.

But from the day of his return, Doman began plotting against the settlers. When Jan van Riebeeck took several Khoikhoi leaders hostage in 1658, shortly after Doman's return from Batavia, his was

the only voice raised in protest – even the hostages themselves were silent, because they enjoyed the food and accommodation.

Doman's first enemy was Krotoa, whom he thought was selling out Khoikhoi interests. According to Van Riebeeck, Doman would taunt her when she passed by: "See, there comes the advocate of the Dutch; she will tell her people some stories and lies and will finally betray them all." Van Riebeeck contemplated locking Doman in the fort and wondered if it might be possible to trick him into going back to Batavia.

Doman tried to channel all trade with the Europeans to the two Khoi groups of the peninsula, which alienated him from the other Khoikhoi. He thus found little support for his plan to attack the fort. But he was successful in mobilising ordinary fighting men against the theft of their grazing near Table Mountain and the way their access to water sources was restricted by the settlers.

When members of the Goringhaiqua or Kaapmans, Doman's clan who lived on the mountain slopes, stole some of the VOC's cattle in early 1659, Van Riebeeck blamed Doman for instigating the theft. He was also blamed for the murder of a free burgher and the theft of his gun.

Van Riebeeck was not wrong. Doman had become the leader of a force consisting of the young men of several Khoikhoi clans who launched guerrilla attacks on the Dutch. He was apparently a good tactician – for one, he told his men to save their most challenging attacks for rainy days because he had heard while in Batavia that white people's guns didn't work in the wet.

Doman's strategy was to destroy the settlers' sources of food rather than kill their men. Hit them where it hurt the most, he argued. His men burned crops and homesteads and stole large numbers of sheep and cattle.

In July 1659, Doman was wounded and some of his men were killed by Abraham Gabbema, the same bailiff who freed Angela van Bengalen. His attackers could see blood spurting from his body, Van

Riebeeck remarked, but he nevertheless managed to escape, "which was a pity, but also good, because it would deter his comrades".

The superior weapons of the Dutch made it a very uneven fight, and eventually the Goringhaiqua and the Gorachouqua withdrew, moving away from the settlement at the Cape. In 1660 the two groups had no choice but to sign a peace treaty with the VOC officials.

Doman's dream of driving the Dutch back across the sea was shattered. He resumed some of his duties as an interpreter, but Khoi clans further from the Cape became more of a threat to the settlers after this.

Doman's demise was recorded on 11 December 1663, but with no reference to the cause of death. He was another Khoi leader whose overseas trip backfired on the Europeans.

And then there's the story of Pegu.

When Simon van der Stel became VOC commander at the Cape in 1679, he employed a young Khoi boy called Pegu (also referred to as Begu) from the Cochoqua clan.

Bizarrely, Van der Stel dressed Pegu in the style of a typical European page of the time: a red uniform with a silver fencing sword, silk stockings, a grey-white wig, a hat with gold braiding and a silver collar with the monogram of the VOC.

Van der Stel appointed a tutor to teach the Khoi boy Dutch, as well as about Christianity and how to behave like a European gentleman.

Five years later a senior VOC official, HA van Rheede, took Pegu over from Van der Stel when he visited the Cape, and took him to Malabar in southern India, where he was commissioner-general. We don't know what young Pegu did when he was in Malabar, but we do know he learnt to speak Portuguese, Sinhalese (spoken today by most Sri Lankans), Bahasa Melayu (the Malaysian language), Tamil and Dutch. There can't be many people in history who can claim fluency in all these languages.

When Van Rheede died in 1691, Pegu was allowed to return home. He was probably the only man in Africa who spoke so many international languages in addition to his native tongue and who had intimate knowledge of both southern India and the southern tip of Africa. He was definitely the only African at the time with a red uniform, a silver sword, a white wig, a hat with silver braiding and a silver collar.

And what did he do when he set foot on Cape soil? He put his red pageboy uniform and all his European clothes in a trunk and donned a traditional Khoikhoi *karos,* which he wore until his death. Bearing only his sword and his collar, he walked inland to reunite with his people, the Cochoqua.

Pegu ended up becoming a chief of his clan. Peter Kolb, a German scientist who was sent to the Cape to make scientific observations, came to know Pegu and wrote that he was astonished at the Khoi chief's knowledge of Christian theology.

François Valentijn, a Dutch clergyman who visited the Cape several times, wrote about meeting Pegu in 1695 and seeing his collar and sword. "I have seen people who had served the Hollanders for twenty years and then went back to their own people," he later wrote.

In 1705, Magistrate Starrenburg recorded an exchange of cattle with Chief Pego in the region of present-day Darling. "Captain Bagu", who brought cattle to the Cape in 1710 as a gift for governor-general Joan van Hoorn, was possibly the same man.

I could find no mention of Pegu's death in the records or books on the period.

3

Eurotrash Gone Native

AFTER THE FIRST EUROPEANS SETTLED AT THE CAPE IN 1652, they were in constant contact – and often conflict – with the Khoikhoi as well as the Bushmen, or San.

By the mid-1700s, mounting pressures in the Cape Colony began pushing white settler groups towards two new frontiers: eastwards to the land of the Xhosa and northwards towards the Gariep (formerly Orange) River, where the new arrivals encountered Sotho/Tswana people.

The interaction on the eastern frontier, which included several wars of dispossession, had a major impact on future political developments in southern Africa. It was here that the first group of South Africa's indigenous farmers, the Xhosa, lost their independence. From this region, too, the Dutch/Afrikaans farmers eventually left for the interior in a migration they called the Great Trek.

In the second half of the eighteenth century, people of mixed Khoi, slave and white blood also started drifting north from the Cape Colony towards the Gariep River. They called themselves Basters (literally, "bastards"), but later many adopted the collective identity of Griqua, derived from the Khoi Charigurikwa clan.

The area around the Gariep became a rough, mostly lawless neighbourhood, peopled by the Griqua, the Khoikhoi (mostly called the Korana or the Oorlams in this area), the Bushmen, the Sotho/

Tswana and a few eccentric white frontiersmen. Cattle rustling was the favourite pastime.

The other significant human ingredient in the mix on both the eastern and northern frontiers was the white Christian missionaries.

These are the unusual stories of three European men who ventured into these regions in the last years of the eighteenth century and influenced history in their own peculiar ways.

Herr Jan Bloem, Chief of the Springboks

Jan Bloem was born in the state of Thuringen in the centre of Germany. We don't know what his real name was, but it probably wasn't Jan Bloem – both Jan and Bloem are typical Dutch names and not German at all.

In fact, we know nothing about the man until he landed at Cape Town harbour in 1780. Some sources say he deserted from his ship. He was married when he lived in Cape Town, but we don't know if his wife was a local resident or came with him from Germany. We do know that Bloem murdered her and then had to flee from the law – he actually walked all the way to the Gariep River.

Somewhere south of what is Kimberley today, the near-dead Bloem was captured by a group of Bushmen, but he was rescued by an armed posse of Khoikhoi, the Katse clan of the Korana (sometimes also called the Kora). Bloem was put on a cow and taken to Dikgatlong on the banks of the Vaal River to meet the chief.

Upon discovering that his guest could read and write, the chief appointed Bloem teacher and scribe of the clan and gave him his own kraal, stocked with cattle and sheep. Bloem was so happy that he stayed for some time, even taking a wife from the tribe.

But he must have fallen out with the chief, because 1786 found him near present-day Upington, living with another Korana clan, the Springboks. He married again – his Katse wife had apparently died – and had his first child. Jan Bloem Junior would eventually become more famous and influential than his father.

While he was with the Springboks, Bloem met Petrus Pienaar, a white farmer and renegade former *veldkornet* (field-cornet) in the Hantam. Pienaar persuaded Bloem to look after one of his farms on the Gariep River.

The first indication we have that Pienaar and Bloem were more than simple agriculturalists came late in 1786. The *veldwachtmeester* (a local law enforcement officer) of the Hantam, Adriaan van Zijl, and his brother-in-law, Jan Wiese, went on a hunting trip to the Gariep River. They attacked a Khoi group, the Nuncquinqua, on the Vaal River and stole all their cattle. On their way back, some of the stolen cattle went missing. They followed the spoor all the way to the farm owned by Pienaar, which Bloem was looking after.

Van Zijl and Wiese confronted Bloem. In his book *Forgotten Frontier*, historian Nigel Penn reports their exchange: "Wiese asked Bloem where their cattle were and Bloem replied in words typical of his character. Since they were the only recorded words he ever uttered, they have a brutal poignancy – fitting, almost, to be his epitaph: '*Bin ik jou beeswagter*?' (Am I your cattle's keeper?) This answer was not appreciated by Wiese, who knocked Bloem unconscious, leaving his body senseless on the veld while the Van Zijl gang rounded up their missing cattle and rode off."

This incident did not discourage Pienaar and Bloem. They recruited some fighting men among the Korana and Bushmen and started raiding the cattle of the Tswana groups in the Gariep River area.

Their first victims were the Tlhaping, a peaceful and relatively prosperous Tswana clan who lived on the banks of the Kuruman River. Pienaar and Bloem took all their cattle, more than two thousand animals, impoverishing the Tlhaping for years to come.

Around 1794, Bloem became a full-time professional cattle thief for his own account and was soon one of the richest men on the northern frontier. His cattle wealth meant he could buy horses, guns and ammunition for his men of the Springbok clan, which

made them a formidable force in the region, despite the fact that they were one of the smallest groupings.

But there was more to their military prowess than guns. Bloem and some of his lieutenants figured out a specialised battle style that was revolutionary for its time. The Springbok fighters rode almost right up to the enemy, dismounted, took careful aim, shot their chosen targets, remounted and quickly rode away, putting themselves out of range of warriors armed with assegais. Then they reloaded and repeated the exercise. Fifteen crack shots on horseback could contain more than a hundred Tswana warriors this way and, over the course of an hour or two, kill many dozens of men.

The Springbok clan recognised that it had Bloem to thank for this newfound power and wealth, and elected him as chief.

Bloem persuaded his clan to move with him to the area around present-day Postmasburg, to be closer to the fat herds of the Tswana. He stayed there for a few years, regularly carrying out cattle raids and selling the stolen livestock in the Cape Colony, where he also restocked his arsenal.

Like a veritable African chief, Bloem took twelve Khoikhoi and San wives and fathered many children – seven of them sons. Around 1795, he moved back across the Vaal River to Dikgatlong, where he had recuperated years before, when the Katse had rescued him.

By this time, Bloem thought nobody could stop him and raided not only the Tlhaping, the Tlharo and Rolong clans of the Tswana, but also the other Korana clans in the Gariep/Vaal region.

And then, inevitably, he crossed one bridge too far. He knew Chief Makaba of the Ngwaketse had thousands of cattle in very good condition, and he wanted them for himself. But Makaba had a powerful army, so Bloem first visited his old enemies, the Tlhaping, the Rolong and the Taaibosch Korana, to make peace – and recruit help, of course – with the promise of a share in the rich prize that awaited.

For months the Springboks and their allies were involved in

skirmishes with the Ngwaketse, but without much success. Makaba was familiar with the Springboks' "flying fight" tactics and avoided direct battles with them. But when he sensed it was time to finally deal with Bloem, he laid a trap to lure the Springboks and their leader into a pass between two hills.

According to William J Burchell in his *Travels in the Interior of Southern Africa 1822–1824*, the Ngwaketse "are said to have raised high walls across the passes between the mountains, leaving small openings in them, like gates, which could easily be closed up at the approach of the enemy. Many lay in ambush, while others were stationed on the tops of the mountains, who rolled down great stones upon their assailants. It is not known that he captured a single beast."

Bloem was one of less than a dozen men who survived the Ngwaketse attack. He fled to Taung, where he stopped at a spring to rest and water the horses. He died within hours of drinking water himself. It was rumoured that Chief Makaba had poisoned the spring.

Bloem was far more than a cattle raider, warmonger and innovative militarist. Forging alliances with – and taking wives from – all the tribes and clans in the region had a profound effect on society along the northern frontier.

In his doctoral dissertation at the University of California, *The Griqua, the Sotho-Tswana and the Missionaries, 1780–1840*, prominent South African historian Martin Legassick says of Bloem: "Indeed, despite his raiding activities, Jan Bloem Sr was among the first constructive contributors to the new political order of the frontier zone. The following which he established around him at Blinkklip and Dikgatlong, drawn from among the San, Khoi and Sotho-Tswana, contributed heavily to the mutual acculturation of the area, and should be classified almost as a multi-ethnic fiefdom."

Many researchers have stated that the capital of the Free State, Bloemfontein, was named after Jan Bloem – even Noël Mostert makes this claim in *Frontiers*. But this is almost certainly a mistake.

The city was more probably named after his son, Jan Bloem Junior. Many writers and some historians have confused the two men.

The younger Bloem was one of the most powerful leaders in the Transorangia area during the first half of the nineteenth century, even waging war, with his Tswana allies, against the feared Ndebele leader Mzilikazi. However, the son owed his power and fame in large part to the stature of his father, the German from Thuringen.

The Priest of Smoke and Mirrors

Was he Greek or was he Polish? Could he have been Latvian? Was his name Stephanos or Stephanus? What was his surname?

We're not sure about much of this man's past, but he arrived on the Gariep frontier in about 1800 and became one of the most interesting personalities of the era.

Most historians, including Martin Legassick and Alf Wannenburgh, call him Stephanus and say he was a Pole. But Nigel Penn, who researched and wrote extensively about the area and the time, calls him Stephanos and says he was born in Greece. Curiously, the nineteenth-century traveller William J Burchell said he came from Courland, which is part of Latvia but was indeed under Polish rule from the sixteenth century until Russia assumed control in 1795.

Most writers who mention Stephanos agree that he was living in Cape Town after being shipwrecked en route to the East. Some say he was in jail for forging papers, others that he was caught making counterfeit coins and sentenced to death in the late 1790s. All agree, though, that he told no one on the Gariep frontier what his real surname was. He was simply Stephanos. Or Stephanus.

In 1801, Stephanos arrived at the Reverend Johannes Kicherer's mission station on the Sak River, east of present-day Calvinia. The visitor presented himself as a religious zealot who wanted to help build a church, and Kicherer allowed him to stay overnight. Stephanos stole the missionary's gun and was about to murder him in his sleep when Kicherer woke up and screamed for help.

Stephanos fled with a few Bushmen who lived at the mission, having persuaded them that they were about to be attacked by colonial forces from the Cape. A party of Khoikhoi men loyal to Kicherer caught up with the fugitives and convinced the Bushmen to turn back, but Stephanos escaped, only to be captured soon afterwards by two missionary assistants, Cornelius Kramer and Jacobus Scholtz, who were returning from an expedition and apparently knew Stephanos was a wanted man in the Cape.

Back at the Sak River mission, Kicherer decided not to hold Stephanos and allowed him to leave. He gave him some food and a Bible and advised him to flee to the north.

And so began a new and exciting life for the intrepid European charlatan. "North" meant Stephanos had to walk for weeks on end through arid, dangerous country to the Gariep River, where he could find isolated communities of Khoikhoi. As it happened, he was welcomed by the Oorlams chief Cornelis Kok, into whose kraal he stumbled at Bitterdagga on the Gariep River. The stranger's timing was good: Kok had heard that white missionaries brought stability and other advantages, such as literacy, with their religion, and he was keen to have a resident missionary. Here was a white man with a Bible in his hand: what else could he be?

Stephanos embraced his new vocation with much enthusiasm and creativity. He devised his own religion with elements of Catholicism, Judaism, Islam and liberation politics, built an elaborate church and devised intricate rituals and ceremonies. Stephanos told his congregants that God wanted them to drive all white Christians from their country and return the land to the Khoikhoi. He presented himself as a prophet sent by God. His flock simply had to believe him, because he had the Bible and was the only one there who could read from it.

Stephanos relied on more than his emotional sermons to impress his followers. According to Alf Wannenburgh in *Forgotten Frontiersmen*: "Each morning he would climb to the top of a hill behind the

grove and, in full view of the people below, would disappear in a cloud of smoke, which he contrived by setting fire to gunpowder that he had scattered about him. He would reappear from the smoke with instructions from God which generally required people to increase his own well-being."

Stephanos not only took two wives, but also regularly took young maidens of the clan to his bed as part of his religious rituals.

In *The Reverend Mr Kicherer's Narrative of his Mission to the Hottentots* (as quoted by Nigel Penn in *The Forgotten Frontier*), Kicherer says that Stephanos established his authority

> on the basis of superstition so firmly, that his will had become the law of every individual in the horde, and the most atrocious crimes were committed by him with impunity. Whoever ventured to murmur against his abominable acts of rapine or lust, was sure to be put into the stocks, or to be beaten unmercifully. Stephanos had erected a temple, resting on pillars, with an altar within, on which sacrifices were offered. He had a number of select disciples who, like himself, feigned trances, in which they lay for many hours, and out of which they pretended to awake with messages which they had brought from the angel Gabriel, or from God himself. Did the Impostor wish to gratify his lust, his covetousness, or his revenge? … Cornelis Kok himself, the Chief, who possessed a vast property, was completely devoted to the will of this wretch. He would preach against us also, and we were apprehensive that his doctrine, like that of Mahomet, might widely diffuse its baneful influences among the neighbouring heathen.

It was this last concern that made Kicherer snap into action. He summoned all the men at his mission who had firearms and went to confront Stephanos at Cornelis Kok's headquarters.

It must have been quite a sight. The two white men, each with Bible in hand, stood under a tree screaming at each other for more than an hour. We have only Kicherer's version of events, and he

obviously thought he was the righteous one, with the only legitimate theological argument. He said Stephanos and his followers were not only unconvinced, but became angrier and angrier and threatened violence. "The Impostor himself conveyed to my mind a striking idea of the Chief of Hell," wrote Kicherer. "His eyes rolled and flashed; his tongue moved with incessant volubility, and he strove to vindicate all his atrocities by examples derived from the Scriptures."

And then the good reverend decided that enough was enough. He'd had enough of trying to persuade the Chief of Hell and enough of being Mr Nice Guy. He promptly ended the arguing by ordering his armed men to arrest Stephanos because he was an escaped criminal from the Cape Colony.

From the available sources, I could not figure out why Cornelis Kok and his people, who had followed Stephanos so faithfully, did not come to his rescue. According to Kicherer, Stephanos broke down and confessed that he was wrong and that Kicherer was the righteous one. Kok's people offered no resistance.

Once again Kicherer decided to let Stephanos escape rather than being saddled with him as a prisoner. This time, he encouraged Stephanos to travel down the Gariep towards Namaqualand and the coast, suggesting he could escape the colony on a passing ship.

On his way, Stephanos ran into a man called Engelbrecht, according to some sources a Cape burgher, while others identify him as a colonial official. He recognised Stephanos and tried to arrest him, but Stephanos overpowered Engelbrecht and cut his throat with a blade he concealed in his Bible.

Stephanos then joined another Oorlams group under Jager Afrikaner, again as a prophet sent by God, but this time there was no Kicherer to provide us with an account of what followed. Nigel Penn makes the point in *The Forgotten Frontier* that despite his wayward teachings, Stephanos played an important role in "preparing Jager Afrikaner for Christianity".

Martin Legassick suggests in his thesis that Stephanos may have

incited Jager Afrikaner to attack the Koks, Adam and Cornelis, who declined to protect their prophet. The result was that Adam Kok and his allies defeated Jager Afrikaner in an attack in February 1802, which both Afrikaner and Stephanos survived.

The next time we encounter the name of Stephanos in the writing of the time is in William Burchell's report that he was murdered by members of the Great Namaqua clan.

The Barefoot Hollander

He was a personal friend of the Dutch royal house, a soldier, gambler, philanderer and atheist. He also spoke sixteen languages, was a qualified medical doctor and became one of the most influential early missionaries in South Africa.

There were indeed few more fascinating characters during the early nineteenth century than the Reverend Doctor Johannes Theodorus van der Kemp. He had an impact on virtually every historical figure on the eastern frontier, including Makhanda – whom we will meet in the next chapter – and the rogue trekboer Coenraad de Buys, about whom I wrote extensively in *Of Warriors, Lovers and Prophets.*

Van der Kemp was born in the Dutch port of Rotterdam in 1748 to a prominent and well-connected family. His father was a Lutheran minister and Van der Kemp himself became a close friend of the Prince of Orange.

He studied philosophy at the University of Leiden, and by the end of his studies he could speak sixteen languages, including English, French, German, Italian, Russian, Sanskrit, Arabic and Hebrew.

But instead of becoming a doctor of philosophy, as his parents expected, he joined the Royal Dutch Cavalry and led a dangerous and wild life of licentiousness and debauchery for sixteen years. Then he fell in love with a woman whose social status was far below his own, and when he married her, the displeasure of both the royal house and his own family forced him out of the army. He went

to Scotland to study medicine at the Edinburgh Medical School, returning to the country of his birth as a qualified physician.

But a personal tragedy changed his life dramatically in June 1791: he witnessed his wife and child drowning after a boating accident. Like so many others faced with such a shock, Van der Kemp turned to God. He went back to university and studied cosmology and theology, eventually becoming a Protestant clergyman.

He was clearly as passionate about his new calling as about his earlier life of vice and believed that God had called him to spread Christianity all over the universe. When he read that the London Missionary Society was sending clergymen to Africa, he applied and, having been ordained as a minister of the Church of Scotland, he left for Cape Town in December 1798. With him was another Dutch missionary, Johannes Kicherer, the man who would deal with Stephanos on the Gariep River.

Van der Kemp and the Reverend John Edmonds left Cape Town in May 1799 on their way to the Eastern Cape and arrived at Graaff-Reinet a month later. Van der Kemp believed God had called him to serve the Xhosa and the Khoikhoi on the eastern frontier, and he was determined to travel to Rharabe chief Ngqika's royal kraal, despite the fact that the whole area was tense because of the ongoing conflict between the Xhosa, the Boers and the British colonialists.

Van der Kemp and Edmonds probably set off at just the right time, because a plot to kill them later came to light. The Boers didn't trust them and had contracted four British deserters to do the killing, but the two missionaries left before this plan could be executed. One of the Boers who resented the missionaries' presence on the frontier was Piet Prinsloo, one of Ngqika's confidants.

On their journey to Ngqika's kraal, the two clergymen had to seek refuge in a Boer *laager* on a farm to avoid being slaughtered by a marauding group of the chief's warriors. But eventually they did arrive at Ngqika's Great Place on 20 September 1799 – the first missionaries to cross the Fish River.

Van der Kemp and Edmonds got an icy reception. The chief, dressed in leopard skins with his face painted red, faced them with his councillors and wives, without saying a word. After fifteen minutes the silence was broken when the giant bearded figure of Coenraad de Buys, who was married to the chief's mother, Yese, appeared and spoke to them in Dutch.

Van der Kemp asked the chief's permission to stay and to inform his people about their happiness on earth and in the afterlife. Ngqika and De Buys both told him his timing was terrible, because it was a season of war and insecurity.

But it later proved to have been Piet Prinsloo who poisoned Ngqika's mind against the missionaries, with stories that they were British spies and planned to kill the chief. In the end, De Buys and his wife, who had a strong influence over her son, convinced Ngqika that Van der Kemp was not an enemy and could, in fact, turn out to be an ally of the Rharabe. But the chief's mother later turned against Van der Kemp, whom she began to see as competition in her rainmaking business.

De Buys became a friend and even attended Van der Kemp's sermons. According to Noël Mostert, "Van der Kemp was wholly won over by de Buys, as so many were, even when they knew the cool, hard and ruthless personality that could function behind the lazy smile and charm of this handsome and muscular giant. 'How inexpressibly wonderful are thy ways, O our God,' Van der Kemp exclaimed to his journal, in gratitude for the favour of de Buys. The success of the encounter owed a great deal, however, to the strength of Van der Kemp's own personality. Coenraad de Buys, the Boer-intended 'King of Graaff-Reinet', accustomed to the power of his own personality over others, was impressed by the force, character and powerful individuality of Van der Kemp. He recognised another outsider, one with a form of strength quite different from his own."

Van der Kemp was clearly in his element in the challenging environment, but his colleague, John Edmonds, was not. He became

depressed and afraid, finding the unhygienic life he had to lead abhorrent. He was not "accustomed to live in the Caffree way", Van der Kemp wrote in his journal. Edmonds was beginning to wonder if he hadn't misunderstood God – perhaps God really wanted him to go and work among the heathens in India.

But Van der Kemp's past as a soldier and adventurer, coupled with his zeal to bring God to the heathens, made him ideal for the work he had to do. In fact, he revelled in the hardship to the point of adding to his suffering. Since establishing himself in Africa, he had refused to wear shoes or a hat.

Now that may sound like a quaint thing to do if he were still in Holland, but he lived in the Eastern Cape, where even the Xhosa and the Bushmen wore sandals to protect their feet from the thorns and sharp stones, and where it could get very, very cold in winter.

Equally, the midsummer Eastern Cape sun, at up to forty degrees Celsius, can burn the fear of Satan into you. Remember, the man was a Dutchman, so he probably had very pink skin. Most of the Boers who lived in the area had at least one slave or Khoi ancestor, so the pinkness had been countered somewhat. Still, you would never have found a Boer without a wide-rimmed hat between sunrise and sunset. The fact that Van der Kemp didn't die of sunstroke is probably testament to his good relationship with the Creator.

Chief Ngqika had never set eyes on a white man without a hat. He once asked Van der Kemp directly whether it was his choice not to wear a hat or whether it was God's wish. The missionary didn't hesitate: it was God's wish.

He explained in his journal: "What does it signify to walk barefooted, as I now have done for almost two years, if my feet may be shod with the gospel of peace? What if I had no hat to cover my head, if it may be protected with the helmet of salvation?"

But Ngqika was far too erratic and insecure to make Van der Kemp's stay pleasant, especially since he often feared, as did his friend De Buys, that the chief was planning to kill them both.

Added to that, his mission was spectacularly unsuccessful: during all his time among the Rharabe, his only converts were a few Khoikhoi women. After eighteen months, Van der Kemp fled Ngqika's kraal and, following a long journey during which he almost drowned and his party was attacked by Bushmen several times, he reached Graaff-Reinet.

Van der Kemp immediately started his missionary work among the Khoikhoi of the area. The Boers became very unhappy because he also taught the Khoikhoi to read and write, which most of them could not, and preached an equality of race that the white settlers didn't believe in. When the Boers attacked the town and tried to shoot Van der Kemp in the street, he decided it was probably a good idea to move on.

Van der Kemp and his new partner, the Reverend James Read, moved towards Algoa Bay (present-day Port Elizabeth) and established a new mission station, which they called Bethelsdorp. It was the beginning of unending conflict between Van der Kemp and the Dutch and later the British colonial governments.

The colonialists had many political and ideological problems with the missionaries, but they also thought that Bethelsdorp wasn't a fit place for a European to live. Willem de Paravicini, aide-de-camp to Dutch governor Jan Wilhelm Janssens, was distantly related to Van der Kemp and visited him at Bethelsdorp. In 1803, this is how he described the visit in his *Reize in de Binnen-Landen van Zuid-Afrika*:

> His abode is a miserable little hut built of mud and reeds … I found the old man lying on one of these beds under a covering of sheepskins sewn together and wearing only a rough blue, striped linen shirt, a coarse woollen jacket and trousers. His nobly-formed bald pate was resting on a wooden block covered with sheepskin; his features a sign of the many vicissitudes of his life, of sorrow and of age … I asked him why he preferred such a hard way of life at his age to a comfortable existence befitting

> his means, but soon observed that in spite of his intellectual abilities he showed a strong tendency towards fanaticism. He assured me that he found the company of people nauseating. The task of bringing lost fellow-beings to Christendom had been laid upon him from Heaven, he assured me, and he would fulfil it to the end of his days. He was content to be deprived of all worldly comforts.

James Read described their time at Bethelsdorp as follows: "For many months we had neither bread nor meat. Breakfast and supper was out of the question – a little milk and water for breakfast and tea, perhaps a little sour milk for dinner or some wild roots or berries when the old Hottentot women came home from the fields in the afternoon. But these were among the happiest days of my life."

Read married a young Khoikhoi woman in 1803, and in 1806 Van der Kemp bought the freedom of a black slave woman from Madagascar and married her. This angered the colonial authorities, even their own missionary colleagues, who frowned upon cross-racial marriages.

Tellingly, Van der Kemp named the son he had with his wife "Africanus".

But the conflict with the colonial officials went much deeper. Van der Kemp believed strongly in the equality of all people and ran a consistent campaign against all who mistreated, assaulted or even murdered Khoikhoi workers or servants. His actions included the lobbying of political and religious leaders in London, to the great embarrassment of the local officials.

Equally serious was the difference of opinion over education for the Khoikhoi and, to some extent, even the Xhosa and the slaves. Van der Kemp saw it as part of his calling in Africa to give the indigenous people proper education, the same education as was given to white people. Most whites in the colony, including government officials, believed the indigenous people were "not yet ready" to be educated, that education would "spoil" them and make them "believe

they were Europeans" and "equal to white men" and that it would lead to a shortage of labourers.

Eventually, the constant harassment of colonial officials, the continued ill-treatment of the Khoikhoi, his deteriorating health and the hardships of living in Bethelsdorp got to Van der Kemp and he asked the London Missionary Society to transfer him to a mission in Madagascar.

He was waiting in Cape Town to hear whether his request had been granted when he died on 9 December 1811. He was only sixty-three years old.

Measured against the number of his converts, Van der Kemp's missionary work among the Xhosa wasn't very successful. His work among the Khoikhoi was more fruitful, although Bethelsdorp always remained a miserable place.

But in retrospect, Van der Kemp and his brother James Read played a huge role in setting an example for missionaries coming after them, to fight against the oppression and exploitation of the local people. They established the principle, very much against the *zeitgeist*, that indigenous Africans were the equal on every human level of their white European counterparts.

Van der Kemp and Read also set an example for their successors in providing local inhabitants with good education, despite the objections of the authorities and the white farming communities. Missionary schools in the Eastern Cape, such as Lovedale and Healdtown, produced most of the early liberation figures in South Africa.

Johannes Theodorus van der Kemp was perhaps eccentric – he may even have been a little fanatical and sometimes downright weird – but he was the one early Hollander in Africa who respected the continent and its people.

A century after his death, another Hollander arrived in South Africa. He was also a bright student who studied in Europe and Britain. He also felt compelled to get involved in the affairs of the indigenous people and became the National Party's minister of

native affairs in 1950. He also had strong views on education for black people. He believed it should be tailored to fit their restricted position in the labour market. He was responsible for closing down most of the mission schools and establishing his version of education for black people, called Bantu Education.

His name was Hendrik Frensch Verwoerd, prime minister of South Africa between 1958 and 1966, and widely acknowledged as the architect of apartheid.

4

Black Samson

THE SAMSON – OR PERHAPS RASPUTIN? – OF THE CAPE frontier. Two metres tall, built like a gymnast, with smouldering eyes and hypnotic voice. A man of great passion and intensity who lived off the veld like John the Baptist – and called himself the younger brother of Jesus.

An unusual creature? Certainly. He also came close to changing the history of colonialism in southern Africa by taking on the British colonial army at its main base on the frontier.

He had four names, this man. His father, possibly sensing that the boy wasn't going to be ordinary, called him Makhanda – the One who Grinds the Maize. (His name was also spelled Makanna or Makana by some.)

Makhanda was left-handed, so from his youngest days certain people called him Nxele. Some say it was out of superstition that they didn't want to utter his real name. The Dutch/Afrikaans trekboers translated Nxele and called him Links. The British clearly didn't know that *links* simply means "left", so they called him Lynx.

But Makhanda was no wildcat. He was a full-blooded alpha male lion.

Neither colonial nor Afrikaner historians paid much attention to Makhanda and he is a figure virtually unknown to most South Africans today. But he remains a great hero among older Xhosa-speakers. The commissars of Umkhonto we Sizwe, the liberation army of the African National Congress, used Makhanda as an inspirational figure to fire up their soldiers. In the camps the ANC

maintained in neighbouring states while they were in exile, Christmas Day was celebrated by many as "Makhanda's Day".

In his autobiography *Long Walk to Freedom*, Nelson Mandela tells the story of hearing as a child in the Eastern Cape of both Robben Island and Makhanda: "Robben Island was well known among the Xhosas after Makanna (also known as Nxele), the six foot six commander of the Xhosa Army in the Fourth Xhosa War, was banished there by the British after leading ten thousand warriors against Grahamstown in 1819."

During the debate many years ago on whether Robben Island should get a new name (*robben* is Dutch for "seals"), Mandela suggested it should be renamed Makhanda's Island. Former political detainees on the island sometimes referred to it as the "Makhanda University".

Part of his fame among former islanders was, of course, that Makhanda had escaped from the island in 1820. (The full story of his escape is told in the next chapter.)

Clearly, Makhanda was an extraordinary figure. But to understand his standing in society and why a traditional Xhosa chief who lived two centuries ago would call himself the brother of Jesus Christ, we have to travel back in history.

During most of the eighteenth century, as the Dutch trekboers and later British colonial forces started encroaching on the Eastern Cape, the Xhosa lived east of the Kei River under their popular king, Phalo. But towards the end of that century the unity was disturbed by a *broedertwis* between his two sons, Gcaleka of the Big House and Rharabe of the Right-Hand House. Rharabe and his people later went to live on the other side of the Kei – which is how the Xhosa people were originally divided between the Transkei and the Ciskei, which later became separate "independent" bantustans under the apartheid government.

When Rharabe died in 1787, his grandson and heir, Ngqika, was too young to lead the people. Rharabe's second son and thus uncle

of Ngqika, Ndlambe, established himself as the chief. But Ngqika was barely out of his teens when he started challenging his uncle's authority. The power struggle between the two, in which Makhanda eventually became embroiled, was given further impetus when Ngqika fell in love with – and kidnapped – one of Ndlambe's most beautiful young wives, Thuthula.

Makhanda was not of royal blood. His father was an ordinary commoner and apparently a bit of a loser, as he never accumulated more than one or two head of cattle. When Makhanda was a baby, his parents lived at the mission station in Bethelsdorp and his father later went to work on a trekboer's farm.

Makhanda was still a boy when his father died and he was sent to live in Ndlambe's kraal. His mother lost all interest in him and later abandoned him altogether.

Instead of becoming pathetic and looking for substitute parents, Makhanda's reaction was to leave the kraal and live on his own in the veld. Like John the Baptist of old, he lived on berries and roots and the occasional bird or rodent he could kill.

Makhanda's lengthy solitude and wandering allowed his substantial intellect a lot of time to ponder the big questions of life. He could draw on two sets of philosophies and religious beliefs and practices: the elements of Christianity he picked up from his father and from living on a Christian trekboer's farm, and the Xhosa traditions and beliefs.

There was possibly a third set of influences on Makhanda that he used to formulate his particular brand of evangelism: the Khoi people. They worshipped a god they called Tsui//Goab and they believed there was a rival evil being they called //Gaunab.

The Xhosa didn't have a clear belief in one supreme god and did not believe in the devil. The ancestors were central to the Xhosa belief system, while the Khoi didn't regard them as particularly important.

There is ample evidence that Makhanda had a deep curiosity

about matters spiritual from an early age – he spent many hours discussing Christianity with every white missionary he ever met. It would be strange if he hadn't had similar conversations with Khoi elders he encountered during his wanderings or at Bethelsdorp, where his father once worked.

Most researchers agree that the Khoi had a significant cultural and religious impact on Xhosa thinking and that there was a lot of intermarrying. I'm interested in possible Khoi influence on Makhanda, because it would help explain aspects of his eventual religious teachings.

There is a possibility that Makhanda's connection with the Khoi could have been much stronger than mere conversation. There are suggestions in the historical records, accepted by some researchers as gospel truth, that Makhanda's mother was in fact a Khoi woman from the Winterberg area.

This would explain other facets of Makhanda's story, such as his early contact with the London Missionary Society's eccentric Reverend Johannes van der Kemp, and his parents' presence at Bethelsdorp, the mission station for Khoi people where Van der Kemp was based. It would also help explain Makhanda's alienation from his mother – perhaps a Khoi woman in a Xhosa kraal did not have an easy life.

It seems Makhanda's contact with Van der Kemp continued after his teenage years. Some sources mention that Makhanda and Van der Kemp "found common ground" and exchanged gifts. Van der Kemp, who insisted on living in a typical Xhosa hut, ate Xhosa food and refused to wear shoes or a hat, was the first Christian missionary in the region.

Makhanda later married a sister of a prominent Khoi chief, Hans Trompetter – the same Trompetter who would help him escape from Robben Island. Apart from his "political" marriage to a niece of Chief Ndlambe, Makhanda's other wives were Bushman or San women.

In his famous book on the early years of the Xhosa people,

Frontiers, Noël Mostert says: "The biblical images he [Makhanda] collected fused in his mystical imagination with the visions and fantasies that crowded into his mind during his lonely wanderings through the bush, where he lived off the wild, and developed his messianic sense of self and purpose."

Makhanda returned from his wanderings to undergo the traditional Xhosa initiation, and it was after this that he started to draw attention to himself with his revolutionary views and strange beliefs.

Makhanda didn't just talk about his beliefs when asked, but became an energetic proselytiser and crusader, addressing gatherings and seeking out chiefs and elders in order to influence them.

His audiences found his performances spellbinding, but his messages were in conflict with what they and those before them had believed for centuries. He blamed the Xhosa people's sinful behaviour rather than the wrath of the ancestors for the droughts, conflict and diseases threatening them. But the Xhosa never believed in "sin" in this way; this was a Christian notion.

Makhanda even refused to eat any prepared food because it had been dirtied by the sinful hands of those who cooked it. He stopped drinking milk and advised others to do the same. This was like telling Italians to stop eating pasta, or forbidding Afrikaners from having a braai.

His crusade was against polygamy, adultery, witchcraft, alcohol abuse and the great pastime of ox racing – gambling, I suppose.

To preach against polygamy and the drinking of milk was simply outrageous – looking for trouble, actually. These practices lay at the heart of Xhosa culture and spirituality.

At one point, a number of people who listened to one of his fiery sermons decided this was too much. They subdued the giant, tied him up and were about to throw him into a huge fire they had prepared.

But then a man with the name Qalanga, possibly an elder or a headman of some sort, stepped in and convinced the men to let Makhanda go. He was deeply struck by Makhanda's physical beauty,

his passion, his charisma and his forceful presence. Qalanga took Makhanda to Chief Ndlambe, who quickly became mesmerised by the messianic prophet.

Makhanda claimed that his life was saved by Christ's personal intervention and used this incident to strengthen his message. Unusually, Ndlambe installed Makhanda in his own Great Place as a chief in his own right.

Makhanda's name for God or the Creator was Mdalidipho, whose son Tayi (or Taayi) was killed but came to life again. He also told the biblical stories of the Creation, the Fall of Man, the Great Flood, the Crucifixion and the Resurrection. He introduced himself as the younger brother of Jesus Christ, but on occasion, when he talked to missionaries, he also called himself the son of Jesus.

In his book *Diviners and Prophets among the Xhosa*, Mongameli Mabona says Makhanda also talked about the "All-Mother, *umfazi omabele made/umfazi obele lide* (the woman with the long breasts/ the woman with the long breast)".

During these early years before 1818, Makhanda saw himself as a colleague of the white missionaries and loved spending time with them. He could speak English as well as Dutch/Afrikaans from the time he was a young man.

Makhanda also spent many hours conversing with the chaplain of the British forces at Grahamstown, former missionary Van der Lingen. According to Thomas Pringle's 1835 publication, *Narrative of a Residence in South Africa*, the chaplain complained that Makhanda confused him with his "metaphysical subtleties" and his "mystical ravings".

In 1816, the Reverend James Read and his colleague Joseph Williams eagerly embarked on a great trip across the Fish River to meet the famous Makhanda who, they had heard, was such a firebrand Christian preacher. Makhanda greeted them with tears in his eyes and invited them to spend time at his Great Place, by now ten substantial kraals with large numbers of cattle.

Noël Mostert reports that the dialogue went like this after Makhanda had asked Read whether they'd had something to eat and they said they had not.

> "I have no cattle, only those of my father. Do you know my father?"
>
> "Who is your father?"
>
> "Taay is my father. *You* call him Jesus Christ. I call him Taay."
>
> "Well, I hope I know him!"
>
> "Do you know *me*?"
>
> "Only from report."
>
> "Well, you will know me tomorrow by noon."
>
> A fat heifer was brought forward.
>
> "That is for you to kill," Nxele said, "because you are my father's children. The Xhosa do not know my father; they will not listen to his word; but they will have to burn!"

The next day, Read and Williams had the opportunity to see Makhanda the evangelist perform at a Sunday service attended by about a thousand people. They were stunned at his remarkable oratory and captivating presence. It was a real fire-and-brimstone sermon warning the Xhosa people of God's wrath if they didn't change their ways.

Read was disturbed by what he heard. Makhanda's brand of religion was a combination of bits of Christianity with "some of the superstitious beliefs of his countrymen," he remarked, and "in his own wild fancies he framed a sort of extravagant religious medley".

After I wrote a short piece about Makhanda in an Afrikaans newspaper early in 2008, a reader, fascinated by the story, asked whether I had considered that Makhanda could have suffered from a personality disorder such as bipolarity, schizophrenia or an extreme form of narcissism. I wrote back and warned against ascribing eccentric behaviour to some form of psychological dysfunction. Perhaps he had touched a nerve – I have, after all, been called "Mad

Max" by many ... Nevertheless, I advised my correspondent to read the full story in this book and then make up his mind.

I noticed that even Jeff Peires, the Eastern Cape academic and politician who has done remarkable work on Xhosa history, commented in his book *The House of Phalo*: "While still a young man he [Makhanda] began to exhibit the hysterical symptoms associated with the initial calling of a diviner, but to an exaggerated degree." Read remarked that he had been told that Makhanda "seems to have been a peculiar person from a child".

I have read most if not all references to Makhanda in old and recent books and in letters and documents of the time, preserved in the Cape Archives. Here's what I think.

Most missionaries and colonial officials with whom Makhanda came into contact thought he was a bit of a nut case. They joked about him, but they also feared him because of his powerful physique and presence and his advanced intellect.

There is reason to believe that the missionaries dismissed him as a freak because he embraced Christianity without being introduced to it by one of them. Most of them were outraged by his claim to be the brother or son of Jesus Christ.

There is no evidence anywhere that Makhanda actually believed he was the physical, biological brother or son of Christ. He most definitely did not see himself as Christ's equal.

It is not hard to imagine that this could have been Makhanda's interpretation of the custom among Christians to talk about "the Christian family", of being the "children of God" or addressing each other as "brother" and "sister". In fact, he told Read and Williams that they were also "my father's children".

He certainly did see himself as special and as a chosen emissary of God to change the ways of his people. And we know he saw no reason why the white missionaries from Europe should arrive in Africa and assume they were to be the indigenous people's spiritual leaders, when there were strong spiritual leaders such as himself.

Not long after his death, another African chief also found the company of white missionaries interesting and some of their ideas helpful, but also refused to accept their spiritual leadership and never allowed their religion to replace his people's natural spirituality. He was King Moshoeshoe, founder of the Basotho nation, who had a close association with the French missionaries Eugéne Casalis and Thomas Arbousset, but never converted to Christianity himself.

I think we should assume that it is likely that Makhanda called himself the brother or son of Jesus only in the spiritual sense, and perhaps to indicate the leadership role he saw for himself.

I could find no reference to Makhanda ever talking about his formal conversion to Christianity. Most committed Christians point out the day they were "saved", "reborn" or "accepted Jesus as their saviour". Makhanda never talked about this. His Christianity was something he grew into, something he developed philosophically. In the same way, he grew out of it during the last years of his life, and as would become clear, the true stature of the man was revealed only after he stopped trying to please the white missionaries.

There is no doubt that Makhanda was an extraordinary man: a leader and a thinker, someone with a strong sense of self, who was not afraid to go against the convention of the day. He lived during a crucially important time: the first encounter between the European colonials and the Bantu-speaking farming groups of southern Africa. It resulted in the end of indigenous peoples' independence and freedom on the subcontinent, and almost two hundred years of white domination.

I believe we should consider the possibility that Makhanda instinctively sought to somehow serve as a bridge between the traditional Xhosa culture and the new civilisation his people encountered with the arrival of the first trekboers and British officials; that he tried to bring the two worlds together so his people could make sense of it.

Mongameli Mabona appears to concur with the view that Makhanda's philosophies were aimed at preserving the peace. He

writes that Makhanda "was acutely aware of the confrontational situation between the Christians (the whites) and the Xhosa. It was his earnest intention at this point to avoid the outbreak of hostilities."

For a number of years, Makhanda embraced the European missionaries and established a civil, sometimes even cordial relationship with the British colonial officers and officials. It is almost as if he wanted to prevent what must have seemed like an inevitable clash between native and coloniser; as if he believed his people would benefit if they borrowed some elements from the cultures, beliefs and technologies of the new arrivals.

Unfortunately for him, the European colonialists, including most of the missionaries, simply saw him and his people as primitive, inferior beings that had to be treated, at best, like children and, at worst, like vermin. And as Makhanda began to realise the futility of a policy of constructive engagement with the foreigners, he slowly turned against them and became their worst nightmare.

But back to Makhanda's first meeting with missionaries Read and Williams. After the Sunday service, Chief Ndlambe also arrived at Makhanda's Great Place to meet the two visitors. He knew, as did Makhanda, that the missionaries had to decide where to be based.

As was the case with other chiefs and kings in southern Africa during the early part of the nineteenth century, there was a certain prestige to having a European mission station attached to your headquarters. It was good for trade and good for relationships with the colonial powers. Above all, Ndlambe and Makhanda wanted to prevent the missionaries from joining their great rival Ngqika, whom they saw as a colonial collaborator. Makhanda thought his Great Place would have been an obvious choice, seeing as he was the first man in the region to embrace Christianity.

But the missionaries had not come to consult. The colonial authorities in Cape Town had already decided that the mission station would be attached to Ngqika. They built their station on the banks of

the Kat River, about twenty kilometres from Ngqika's Great Place. It was the first sanctioned European colonial outpost in Xhosa territory.

The missionaries' decision was not only a blow to Ndlambe and Makhanda, but also marked a turning point in Makhanda's thinking and his strategies. It was the beginning of a process that would end with him as the British colonial authority's most bitter enemy.

Makhanda was drifting back to the ways of his people. He started painting his body with clay for ceremonial purposes and began joining in the ritual dancing. Most obviously, after campaigning against polygamy for so long, he took three wives: two Bushman women and Ndlambe's niece.

At the end of November 1816, Ngqika and his entourage arrived at the mission station in a great hurry. He said he had come to warn Joseph Williams, who was in charge of the mission station, that Makhanda was on his way and planned to humiliate the missionary in front of a large group of people.

Makhanda did indeed arrive the very next day, but clearly not to humiliate Williams. It seems Ngqika had not gone to warn Williams after all. The two chiefs were actually looking for an opportunity to square up against one another, because it had been clear for some time that a showdown was inevitable.

Makhanda threw down the gauntlet when he gave the paramount chief of the Rharabe a vicious tongue-lashing with Williams, Ngqika's entourage and hundreds of Makhanda's followers and other curious onlookers as witnesses.

Ngqika, an insecure and unpleasant man, felt threatened by this commoner chief's charisma and stature, but also because Makhanda was seen as a prophet and a religious leader with special connections to the white colonial powers. His answer now was to find his own Christian prophet, a young mystic by the name of Ntsikana.

Ntsikana had a vision as a young man when he was sitting at his cattle kraal. A strong ray of light came from above and shone like a spotlight on his favourite ox, an animal he named Hulushe.

He was due to take part in a big dance that morning and his body was already adorned in red clay. But every time he tried to join the dance, a whirlwind would suddenly spring up. He never danced again, and on his way home he walked into a river and washed all the clay off, an act interpreted as wanting to rid himself of all impurity.

It was the beginning of his new life as a prophet. The missionary Van der Kemp had made a strong impression on him when he was still a boy, but after that he had a lot of contact with Joseph Williams – in fact, he was one of only four Xhosa converts that Williams could claim.

Ntsikana offered his "services" to Ndlambe, but since the latter already had a relationship with Makhanda, he wasn't interested. So Ntsikana joined Ngqika and almost immediately became the chief's tool with which to counter Makhanda.

Ntsikana's theology was closer to conventional Christianity and he regularly lambasted Makhanda for being a "false prophet" who was deliberately misleading the people. Makhanda was wrong in saying God was on earth; he was in heaven and his name wasn't Mdalidipho, but Thixo. He pleaded with the Xhosa to submit to the will of Thixo and to refrain from all conflict.

But Ntsikana also did some serious sucking up to his sponsor, Ngqika. The biggest favour he could do for Ngqika was to undermine Ndlambe and question Makhanda's legitimacy as a chief. God appointed chiefs by birth, Ntsikana preached, and Makhanda therefore was wrong to claim he was one.

The closer Ntsikana moved to conventional Christianity, the further away from it Makhanda moved. He was turning against the white settlers and colonialists and started espousing confrontation and war. He became what was known as a "war-doctor".

There were not one but two gods, he now started saying. Mdalidipho was the black man's god and Thixo was the white man's god. White people had killed Thixo's son, who then drove them from their home country into the sea, from where they came to invade the land of the Xhosa.

But Mdalidipho was a more powerful god than the white man's god, Makhanda told his followers, and would help the Xhosa defeat the white invaders and those who collaborated with them. The Xhosa should stop praying like the missionaries and start dancing and having sex so that black people could multiply, he said.

The competition between Ngqika and Ndlambe came to a head in October 1818. Makhanda was Ndlambe's chief general and soon proved his military genius.

Makhanda sent a group of his men to round up a large number of cattle belonging to one of Ngqika's chiefs in order to provoke him into coming down from his Great Place onto the plains below the Amatola mountains. As the amaNgqika approached the valley, they saw a number of small units of Ndlambe's army, and charged.

But these soldiers had been sent by Makhanda as decoys, and as Ngqika's men charged past, Ndlambe's main army stood up and began a slaughter never seen before or since in Xhosa history. In his book *Battles of South Africa*, Tim Couzens states that it was "more than likely" that these tactics came from Mdushane, son of Ndlambe and nominal commander of his troops. If that is true, it would make one wonder why Mdushane played such a minor role in future battles.

Ndlambe's warriors killed most of Ngqika's men, pursued the fleeing survivors and made sure that every wounded soldier was killed and their beads and ornaments taken. Ngqika survived and fled to the north, pleading for British assistance.

Noël Mostert says this about the Battle of Amalinde, as it became known: "The merciless, unrelenting ferocity with which this battle was pursued to its methodical conclusion by firelight indicated as well as anything could the hatred that Ngqika had cultivated against himself through the failings of his own character, his greed, ruthlessness, cruelty, and his collaboration with the British."

Two weeks or so before this battle, a new commander was sent to the British military outpost at Grahamstown. He was Lieutenant-

Colonel Thomas Brereton of the Royal African Corps, whose previous posting was as lieutenant-governor of Senegal and its adjacent slave island, Gorée.

Brereton was ordered to put together an army to punish Ndlambe and Makhanda. On 1 December 1818 this force, consisting of Ngqika's surviving soldiers, a number of trekboers under Andries Stockenström, a group of Khoi soldiers and, of course, members of the British army, left for Ndlambe's Great Place.

Makhanda wasn't a fool; he wasn't going to attack this well-armed commando. So the amaNdlambe hid with their cattle among the dense bush of the Keiskamma valley.

Brereton's answer was crude and vicious: he fired his cannons indiscriminately into the bush. This tactic didn't hurt the people, but it caused several cattle stampedes. Brereton's force captured more than twenty thousand head of cattle – virtually all that Ndlambe and his people owned. Apart from the symbolic impact of being rendered cattle-less, the loss also meant no milk or meat for the tribe. To add insult to injury, some cattle were given to Ngqika, others to the trekboers who served in Brereton's force.

Brereton's raid was a huge mistake, one that had a long-term impact on the politics and attitudes of the Eastern Cape. Within a year the Xhosa had taken back most of the Zuurveld (the area between the Bushmans and Fish rivers), white farmers fled in droves as a result of widespread cattle raids on farms, and soldiers travelling in the area were ambushed.

Brereton was allowed to go back to England soon afterwards and he was replaced by Lieutenant-Colonel Thomas Willshire.

The Brereton fiasco was the final straw for Makhanda. In the words of Ensign Charles Lennox Stretch, a young British soldier stationed in the region at the time (whose *Journal of Charles Lennox Stretch* was republished in 1988), "the whole soul of the warrior prophet seems to have been set on revenging the aggressions of the Christians and emancipating his country from their arrogant

control". And that was the Makhanda that lived on in the minds of the Xhosa people for many generations.

Now Makhanda started preparing for something never before contemplated by the Xhosa, or indeed other indigenous groups of southern Africa: a full-on military attack on a colonial garrison, in this case the main British post on the frontier, Grahamstown.

There was another reason why Grahamstown had to be the target of this great assault: the town was named after Colonel John Graham, who was sent to the Zuurveld to "expel the natives". He did this with great enthusiasm and extraordinary cruelty. At the end of his campaign, many of Ndlambe's subjects were dead and thousands more had been left without homes, without food, without land.

Makhanda knew the layout of Grahamstown and he had up-to-date information on how many soldiers were stationed there. Ngqika's interpreter and emissary, Nquka, who was allowed to come and go as he liked in the town, had secretly been recruited as an informant by Makhanda.

Makhanda assembled an army of some ten thousand men from Ndlambe's people, as well as from most of the smaller chiefs supporting him – the biggest Xhosa army ever to go into battle.

Nquka was part of Makhanda's plan. On 19 April 1819, Nquka told Willshire there was something suspicious going on east of Grahamstown, and the commander dispatched a strong patrol to investigate, which meant fewer men in the town to overpower.

On 21 April, Makhanda sent one of his warriors into town with a message for Willshire: "We shall breakfast with you tomorrow morning." Rhodes University history professor Julia Wells believes this message was sent "in accordance with the Xhosa tradition of ensuring a fair fight".

Willshire must have known by now that something was afoot, but he clearly didn't take it seriously, because he rode out on patrol the next morning, only to charge back when he saw large numbers of warriors in the distance.

In almost leisurely fashion, and in broad daylight, the warriors,

all covered in red ochre, were taking up their positions along the ridge overlooking Grahamstown. This gave Willshire time to position his men and plan his defence.

Makhanda himself stood at the end of the ridge, from where he could survey the whole scene. This, he must have thought, was going to be his greatest moment and that of his people. He was going to defeat the mighty British in their own stronghold.

The warriors had to rush down a steep slope, cross a small stream and then run up a gentler slope to the first line of British soldiers.

When Makhanda gave the signal, his men rushed down with spine-chilling cries, ready to destroy the invader enemy. The British soldiers in their scarlet uniforms waited until they were about thirty or forty metres away, then fired their deadly rifles. At the same time, the British artillery fired shrapnel shells over their own soldiers' heads, cutting wide corridors through the warrior ranks.

Some sources claim the artillery was the determining factor, not so much because of its devastation, but because of the huge, bright flashes at the cannon muzzles – something Makhanda couldn't have foreseen. Noël Mostert, for instance, says: "The flashes of the cannon helped to destroy their momentum, which was at that point their principal advantage. On seeing a flash they defensively raised their left arms and cloaks to cover their eyes. It made them a better target for the British infantry line. Their fear of looking at this leaping fire also affected their throwing skill, and their spears fell short. Others fell to their knees and covered their faces."

The Xhosa warriors fought bravely on. Makhanda had gambled from the start on the huge superiority in numbers securing victory for him, and it almost did. The men fighting at the barracks were gaining the upper hand and Willshire's line of infantrymen was close to being overwhelmed.

If the deadly shrapnel shells did not tip the fight in favour of the British, the unexpected arrival of a group of about 130 Khoikhoi hunters at the height of the battle did. Led by one Boesak, a Christian

convert, they were all experienced marksmen. They picked out the commanders and the bravest warriors and shot them down, one by one.

By mid-afternoon, Makhanda realised it was a futile effort and, three hours after the first shot was fired, called off the attack. He had lost many hundreds of men, perhaps even as many as two thousand. The British lost only three men, with five wounded.

After this fateful battle, Grahamstown was named Egazini – Place of Blood – by the local people.

We will never know for sure why Makhanda, a man with a clear talent for military strategy, decided to attack Grahamstown in broad daylight or, for that matter, why he warned the British commander of the attack a day earlier and didn't even try to conceal the deployment of his troops in the hours before the battle.

Willshire and his men did not expect the attack and, right up to seeing the warriors taking up positions along the ridge, did not believe they were under threat. If Makhanda had kept the element of surprise to the end, and if he had attacked at night, the outcome would almost certainly have been different.

If the British had been defeated at Grahamstown on that April afternoon in 1819, it would probably have stopped the ambitious British immigrant scheme that was then in an advanced planning stage. Thousands of British settlers were brought to Albany the very next year.

Makhanda's plan was to capture the British cannons and firearms at Grahamstown and use them for an assault on Graaff-Reinet. South African history would have developed a lot differently if Makhanda's army had won the day.

Perhaps Makhanda really thought he was invincible, or that Mdalidipho would indeed ensure his victory over the European invaders.

Or perhaps he knew instinctively that the defeat of the Xhosa people was inevitable in the end, faced with the colonialists' superior

weapons technology, and that the Battle of Grahamstown was more about symbolism and poetry than real war.

Makhanda fled to the coast with some of his followers. Perhaps his last public statement holds the answer to his secret.

He went to Gompo, a massive overhanging slab of rock on the beach, now known as Cove Rock, just outside East London. He told his people that he was going to call their ancestors from the sea to help them drive away the white colonialists.

But, he added, the ancestors would rise only once he had leapt over a wide split in the rock slab – a jump too far for any human to achieve.

On the day he was supposed to raise the ancestors, a large number of people gathered on the beach to watch him jump and to sacrifice animals to the ancestors. Makhanda just sat there, looking at the gap, not attempting to jump. Late in the afternoon his people started shouting that they were tired, cold and hungry, and that he had to make the leap.

Makhanda continued to merely sit there, deep into the night, not saying a word.

Four months after his attack on Grahamstown, on 15 August 1819, Makhanda walked into the camp of the Boer commander Andries Stockenström at Trompettersdrift and surrendered. Stockenström was so taken with Makhanda's regal presence that he had him stay in one of their wagons and fed him the food the Boers were eating. "To secure him by the wagon chain or thongs I shrank from," he wrote.

At a re-enactment of the Battle of Grahamstown in 2008, the mayor of Makana (as the municipality of the town and the Albany district is now known), Phumelelo Kate, said Makhanda surrendered because he was "accepting accountability for the high numbers of amaXhosa who had been killed in combat".

On 16 October 1819, the following announcement appeared in the *Cape Town Gazette and African Advertiser*:

> The Caffer Chief Lynx arrived in His Majesty's ship Redwing from Algoa Bay on the 10th and was conveyed to Robben

> Island, on the 12th instant, where such arrangements have been made for his future residence, as will afford every comfort and indulgence which his habits may require, and which may be consistent with the safe custody of his person.

Makhanda was kept in a small house away from other prisoners on Robben Island.

About 140 years later, another controversial, visionary Xhosa-speaker born in the Eastern Cape was also sent to Robben Island and kept away from other prisoners in a small house. His name was Robert Mangaliso Sobukwe, founder and first president of the Pan Africanist Congress.

5

Escape from the Island (*Part 1*)

ANCIENT STONE AGE PEOPLES PROBABLY LIVED ON THE piece of land that is Robben Island today, because during the last Ice Age, which ended about 10 000 years ago, sea levels were a lot lower and the island was linked to the mainland.

But once it became an island, no one set foot on it until after 1488, when the first European sailors arrived at the Cape, because the indigenous people were not seafarers.

From that day forward, the island was used as a place to imprison or isolate people, which meant that for more than three centuries it was also a place from which people planned to escape.

It is the perfect setting for a jail. The closest land is Bloubergstrand, seven kilometres away. The sea is cold and seldom calm, with no guarantee that a shark with a healthy appetite won't be passing by while you're in the waters around the island. In summer the vicious southeaster blows more often than not, and in winter the regular north-westerly gales make even living on the island hard.

That is why not a single prisoner has ever escaped from Robben Island without a boat. But quite a few got away with the help of a vessel.

The first escape I could find in the records was that of five Khoi men who were sent to the island by Dutch settler leader Jan van Riebeeck's administration for assaulting a shepherd. They stole a tiny rowing boat in January 1673 and made it to Bloubergstrand undetected.

There were more escapes in 1716 and 1718 and again in 1746. From the mid-1700s, the authorities started controlling the ships and boats visiting the island after some foreign ships picked up prisoners to replace their depleted crews, while others left their rowing boats unattended on the island, presenting prisoners with a huge temptation.

But the biggest and most famous escape happened in 1820 and involved our hero from the previous chapter – Makhanda, the Xhosa "war-doctor".

He was a man who loved the open spaces; indeed, he had once led a nomadic existence, living off the veld. After his surrender he was held in leg-irons in small cells. Even before he was put aboard HMS *Redwing* he had already tried twice to escape. Reports by the authorities indicate that he nearly lost his sanity during his first weeks of confinement on the island.

Makhanda was treated differently from other prisoners and could even determine his own diet. The Cape colonial governor's deputy secretary, Henry Ellis, wrote to the commander at Robben Island, Captain Petrie, on behalf of "His Excellency" (HE) on 11 October 1819:

> As the Caffre Chief can in no respect be considered on a similar footing with persons sent to Robben Island under judicial condemnation it has appeared advisable to HE that some separate apartment should be provided for him, and with this view, a small tenement in the garden of Mr Murray has been hired for the future residence of the Chief. Mr Murray has undertaken to have it immediately prepared for his reception; you will therefore, on the arrival of the prisoner, adopt such measures for preventing escape from thence as the situation may require.

Before we investigate Makhanda's actual escape, let's meet the dramatis personae of this extraordinary event.

There were eighty-two prisoners on the island at the time. Apart from Makhanda, eighteen other Xhosa men were being held as prisoners of war. Most were captured in the Zuurveld, the land between the Bushmans and Fish rivers, which had been declared a no-go area for Xhosa males after Ndlambe had been defeated. The Xhosa prisoners were not tried in a court or before a tribunal, so there are no official records containing personal information about them.

Two of the ringleaders of the escape were veterans of the struggle against colonial occupation: the Khoi leaders Dawid Stuurman and Hans Trompetter, whose sister was married to Makhanda. Stuurman had escaped from the island once before, but was recaptured and sent back in December 1819.

Three of the escapees were Khoisan servants who had run away from their employees and formed gangs that robbed and stole. They were Jan Swart, Abraham Leenderts and a man known only as Kiewet.

There were also two slaves who had become notorious in the Cape for escaping and leading gangs of other runaway slaves. Instead of surnames, and like so many other slaves, Absalon and Saloman merely had the suffix "of the Cape" appended to their names. They were probably of East Indian origin or descent and were part of the escape planning committee. The slave Jan of Mozambique was an enthusiastic participant, while another Mozambican, Bamboe, was taken along against his will.

Two white men, William Holmes and Johan Smidt, featured prominently in the escape plan. I could find no information on Holmes, other than that he was British. Smidt was a soldier of the Dutch East India Company who worked as a court orderly in Cape Town until he was convicted of fraud and sent to Robben Island.

The escape itself is documented in detail in *Rebellion and Uproar: Makhanda and the Great Escape from Robben Island*, a booklet by Julia Wells, published by the University of South Africa Press as part of the Hidden Histories Series. Her account relies mostly on court

records and other documents and letters kept at the Cape Archives Repository.

The operation started at daybreak on 9 August 1820. Smidt overpowered a guard outside his cell door, took his rifle and ammunition and then freed the other men. The prisoners fought their way through the guards' sleeping quarters, seizing more weapons and ammunition as they went. Several soldiers were badly wounded and, later in the day, one died.

Some of the men used a bayonet to gouge a hole in the wall, through which they escaped. Hans Trompetter led a group in an attack on another room full of sleeping soldiers. A firefight between convicts and soldiers ensued outside, the convicts at one point driving cattle in front of them as shields.

Trompetter and fourteen of the Xhosa prisoners raced to the house where Makhanda was kept. After firing only two shots, his guards surrendered. The twenty-four escapees then seized four boats belonging to John Murray, who held the concession to run a whaling station on the island from 1806. One boat was smashed on the rocks as some of the prisoners clambered aboard, while in another Makhanda, Stuurman, Trompetter and three Xhosa prisoners began rowing feverishly towards the mainland.

The fact that the group risked failure by going to liberate Makhanda, who had no part in the planning, indicates that the escape was at least in part an act of political resistance. The solidarity between the two Khoi leaders and the Xhosa prisoners, as well as the commitment of these two men to Makhanda, must be seen as significant. Too often it is stated that the Khoikhoi and the Xhosa were sworn enemies.

In fact, the participation of Holmes, Smidt and the slaves makes the August 1820 escape the first act of "non-racial" resistance against oppression in South Africa – something that only really caught on during the struggle of the United Democratic Front from 1983.

In her analysis, Professor Wells says: "This massive escape from

Robben Island deserves to be seen as an important chapter in the resistance history in South Africa. The main body of support for the highly risky exercise came from the eastern frontier prisoners, all of whom were on Robben Island because of their refusal to cooperate with colonial rule ... It can hardly be seen as a coincidence that Stuurman, Trompetter and several other Xhosa escapees all rallied around Makhanda and travelled in the same boat as him."

The boat with Holmes, Kiewet and others capsized in rough seas. Holmes drowned and Kiewet was recaptured soon after. Smidt's boat made it safely to Melkbosstrand and all his men got away, only to be captured one by one over the following two weeks.

Makhanda's boat capsized in the surf at Bloubergstrand. Makhanda was apparently clinging onto the rocks, shouting encouragement to the others. Trompetter and Stuurman made it to the beach, but were recaptured two days later.

And Makhanda? The story in Cape Town was that he had drowned – a missionary actually reported hearing that his body had washed up. But some Xhosa sources claim he made it to the beach, where he was shot by British soldiers who then threw his body into the sea.

Back on the eastern frontier, people believed for decades afterwards that he had survived and would return home. Wells reports that Chief Ngqika "pestered missionaries for information on Makhanda's whereabouts, years after the escape".

His death was never announced officially and his body was never produced for burial. It was not until fifty-three years later that his family buried his personal possessions and ornaments at his kraal.

Perhaps it is fitting that a life that was such an enigma should end so mysteriously.

We do know what happened to Smidt and Trompetter. They were convicted of mutiny, hanged and decapitated. Their heads were displayed on spikes on Robben Island.

Dawid Stuurman, who prevented John Murray's foreman from

being killed during the escape, was banished to Australia, where he died seven years later.

Following the escape, Murray was told to leave the island and take all his boats with him. After that, no fishing boats were allowed to beach on the island, and escape became virtually impossible, although that did not prevent subsequent generations of prisoners from trying.

6

Breastfeeding the Warriors

It has never been easy for a woman to be a ruler of men – not now, and especially not during the eighteenth and nineteenth centuries. Equally, it was never easy anywhere in the world, but particularly not in patriarchal Africa.

So when a woman served successfully as a chief or head of a nation, people or clan, one can be sure that she was no ordinary human being. One definite sign that such a woman was truly formidable is that she would be demonised by men in a desperate effort to minimise her stature.

South Africa had such a woman in the early nineteenth century. Mantatisi was her name. After just a few years as chief of the Batlokoa, she was rumoured all over the subcontinent to have had a hunchback and only one eye in the middle of her forehead.

Fearful and jealous, insecure men told the story that she breastfed all her troops herself and commanded millions of bees which she sent ahead of her army to soften their targets. Some groups, far away from where she operated, imagined that they had battles with her army and wrote these into history. Soon her people became known as "the Mantatees", which also became the name people in the region started giving to any aggressive, marauding group.

The truth is that she was exceptionally beautiful, with a regal posture, and was a caring mother. She was also a military genius and a cunning politician, who kept her small clan together and saved

them from annihilation during one of the most traumatic and bloody periods in the history of southern Africa.

Much of what we know about Mantatisi was written by David-Frédéric Ellenberger, a Swiss missionary working among the Basotho in the heart of South Africa during the mid-nineteenth century. In his book *History of the Basuto, Ancient and Modern*, published in 1912, he says he saw it as part of his calling to find out everything he could about the Basotho, their history and traditions, and write it down. His grandson, Paul, later wrote that Ellenberger refused to talk to local inhabitants about God before they told him "about yourself, your father, your grandfather, your forefathers as far as you can go". Ellenberger also interviewed elders at length and recorded family lineages stretching as far back as 1200.

Another major source of information was provided by two earlier French missionaries stationed with the Basotho king Moshoeshoe. Eugéne Casalis and Thomas Arbousset joined the Basotho while Mantatisi was still alive.

What all three of these missionaries and other writers did was record the oral histories given to them by the people who had first-hand knowledge of the stories surrounding Mantatisi or had heard them from their parents and grandparents. We have ample evidence that these accounts, if recorded without or with little prejudice and with some understanding of the people who told them, are mostly remarkably accurate.

So here's the story of Mantatisi – whose name was also spelt Manthatisi, Mantathisi and MaNtatisi – chief of the Wild Cat People, the Batlokoa.

She was born in 1781 in the Wilge River valley in the district of present-day Harrismith. Her father was Mothaha, chief of the Basia, and he named her Monyalue. The Basia were a Sesotho-speaking clan who had moved from the Magaliesberg area more than a century earlier. They were joined in the eastern Free State in the early 1700s by another Sesotho-speaking clan, the Batlokoa. The

two ruling families became closely connected due to frequent intermarriage.

Ellenberger recorded that Monyalue was "a handsome, intelligent girl with a pleasant manner. She was tall and, in her youth, slim and graceful. She was of light brown complexion which was not unpleasing to the Batlokoa, perhaps by way of contrast, for their own colour is exceptionally black."

Monyalue's light complexion could simply have been a genetic quirk, but it is more likely that it was due to some Bushman (San) blood in her family. The eastern Free State and the foothills of the Drakensberg were home to relatively large numbers of Bushmen during that time and intermarriage with Bantu-speakers did occasionally take place.

Monyalue married Mokotjo, chief of the Batlokoa and also her father's sister's son, who was brought up among the Basia. Monyalue and Mokotjo's first child was a girl, whom they called Ntatisi. From the day of the child's birth in 1801, as was the custom of the time, Monyalue was called Mantatisi – Mother of Ntatisi. Later, her people sometimes also referred to her as Mosayane, the Little Woman, which was a term of respect and endearment and did not refer to her physical size.

In 1804, Mantatisi and Mokotjo had a son, Sekonyela, and a few years later another, whom they named Mota.

But in 1813 Mokotjo died of an unknown disease. His natural successor, his first-born son Sekonyela, was only nine years old and could obviously not become chief at an uneasy time that would seriously challenge the leader of a vulnerable clan like the Batlokoa.

Several Tlokoa elders and more than one of the Batlokoa's enemies were ready to take advantage of the leadership vacuum.

We don't know how she did it, but Mantatisi stepped firmly into her dead husband's shoes and established herself as chief until Sekonyela would be old enough to assume his responsibilities.

In a paper titled "A Comparative Study of Strategy in Bantu Tribal

Warfare During the 19th Century", published in the *Military History Journal*, Dr Peter Becker writes that "members of the Royal house of the Wild Cat People sought to kill her and also to prevent her minor son, Sekonyela, from becoming the new chief of the clan". Other sources suggest that her brother-in-law, Sehalahala, believed he was the designated ruler and vehemently opposed her.

The fact that she was born into the Basia clan definitely counted against Mantatisi, but her gender was obviously a greater difficulty. Still, there were a few other examples of female chiefs and powerful leaders in southern Africa during the pre-colonial period. Shaka's aunt Mnkabayi (senior sister of his father, Senzangakhona) is one example; Midambuze, daughter of the Pedi chief Dambuze, is another. Two generations earlier, says historian Elizabeth Eldridge in her book *A South African Kingdom: The Pursuit of Security in 19th Century Lesotho*, the Batlokoa chief Tsotetsi (born in 1735) died while his heir was too young to rule, and his widow Mamohlalo proclaimed herself regent.

David Sweetman states as fact in *Women Leaders in African History* that Mantatisi's mother-in-law, Mmamane, had also ruled the Batlokoa in Mokotjo's name for a short period. And then, of course, there was the Rain Queen, Modjadji of the Balobedu.

For the first few years after she took power, Mantatisi's enemies constantly challenged her authority, even threatening her life and that of her son. But she held on and became stronger and stronger in her position, and by the time the Wild Cat People faced their first major military challenge, she was firmly ensconced.

In 1817, Mantatisi's warriors attacked a Hlubi clan, an Nguni-speaking group living on the other side of the Drakensberg, and captured most of Chief Zwedi's cattle. This conquest and sudden new wealth solidified Mantatisi's reputation as a strong leader, and a few months later, another amaHlubi chief, Motsholi, brought his two thousand followers and their cattle to join her people, because he was being harassed by other groups. Mantatisi's fame was beginning to spread.

But eventually, it came time for the real heir to the Batlokoa chieftaincy, Sekonyela, to be circumcised and initiated. Mokotjo had told Mantatisi that his brothers from his father's second wife, Moepi and Sehalahala, nearly killed him when he was undergoing initiation because they didn't want him to become chief. Mokotjo said Sehalahala (Moepi had died by then) was likely to want to kill his heir, Sekonyela, so that he himself could rule.

Mokotjo's suspicions were correct, because Sehalahala connived behind Mantatisi's back to get Sekonyela to join the new batch of Batlokoa initiates who were about to be circumcised (probably in 1818).

When Mantatisi heard about this, she sent some of her trusted soldiers to remove her son by force. She then accompanied him to the main kraal of the Basia, where she entrusted supervision of Sekonyela's circumcision and initiation to her brother, Letlala. (Mokotjo was also circumcised by the Basia.) Sekonyela thus got the circumcision name of Lentsa, meaning "he who was withdrawn", and his circumcision mates were therefore called Mantsa.

The Batlokoa elders were obviously angry that their future chief was circumcised by another clan. Sehalahala made the most of this and stoked the fires of protest against Mantatisi, even among neighbouring clans and chiefs.

As Sekonyela's paternal uncle, Sehalahala had to provide the branches with which the initiation hut was to be built. He did have the branches cut, but left them in the veld instead of taking the wood to Letlala, Sekonyela's maternal uncle. Letlala accused him of wanting to bewitch Sekonyela and the other initiates, and a seething Sehalahala decided to leave with his adherents and cattle to join one of Mantatisi's opponents.

Mantatisi suspected Sehalahala was planning to attack her, which he was, and mobilised her warriors in time. Sehalahala then attacked a small group loyal to Mantatisi, the Malakeng, instead, but he was driven back and his chief adviser killed. He fled the area and Mantatisi occupied his village.

Meanwhile, the amaHlubi chief who had joined her earlier, Motsholi, had fallen out of her favour. She had given him a kraal and land in one of the fertile valleys under her jurisdiction, and he came to her kraal regularly to pay his respects. Mantatisi noticed that he brought his own food on these occasions and thus refused to eat meat sacrificed to the spirit of her husband and former chief of the Batlokoa, Mokotjo. Mantatisi took offence, and when she heard that Motsholi was talking about establishing an independent chieftainship, she decided to act.

But she was pre-empted by her son Sekonyela, fresh out of initiation school. This is also the first indication we have that Sekonyela wasn't going to be the wise and sensible leader his mother was. Sekonyela and his initiation mates, the Mantsa, attacked Motsholi and his elders while they were engaged in a *lekhotla*, or council meeting, and killed them all on the spot.

Sekonyela wanted the brass plate that Chief Motsholi wore around his neck, and cut off his head, carrying it away as a trophy. Most of Motsholi's followers fled across the Drakensberg to join the other Hlubi people. Among them was Motsholi's widow, who was the sister of the powerful amaHlubi chief Mpangazitha.

It was Mpangazitha who started a period of great trauma and hardship in the life of Mantatisi and her Wild Cat People.

During the first two decades of the nineteenth century, a number of factors disturbed the existing equilibrium among the Bantu-speaking farmers who moved into southern Africa more than two thousand years ago. Among these factors were prolonged droughts, scarcity of land, pressures of a colonial presence in the Cape and Mozambique, even the trade in slaves and ivory along the Mozambique coast, which brought new pressures and forced social change.

Added to this complex mix were certain strong individuals, like the Nguni-speaking kings Dingiswayo and Shaka, who reacted to these unsettling influences by launching campaigns of military conquest.

This strategy became more concrete when Shaka claimed the Zulu throne in 1816, abolished the age-old custom of initiation, started militarising his society, built up an almost invincible army and absorbed one clan after another into his Zulu kingdom.

In 1822, these upheavals spilled over to the Highveld, home of the Sotho-speakers. Three powerful Zulu-speaking chiefs – Matiwane of the Ngwane clan, Mzilikazi of the Khumalo clan (later called the Matabele, or the Destroyers) and Mpangazitha of the amaHlubi – fled Shaka's army and started attacking the Sotho-speaking groups, opening a vicious cycle of attack and revenge that led to great suffering and famine, lasting several years.

It was during these upheavals, which some call the Lifaqane, that Mantatisi showed her real skills as a leader, a strategist and a military tactician.

Matiwane was uprooted first, and he in turn fell upon the amaHlubi, killing many of them, burning their crops and villages and taking their cattle. Mpangazitha gathered his group of Hlubi adherents and moved into the Wilge River valley, home of Mantatisi's Batlokoa.

Mpangazitha had a special reason for attacking Mantatisi: to avenge the murder by Sekonyela of his sister's husband, Motsholi. As Ellenberger says: "This, of course, may be correct, and doubtless vengeance was not undesired by Pakalita [Mpangazitha], or unwelcome when the chance came; but the line of flight of a fugitive tribe, with an enemy like the terrible Matuoane [Matiwane] at their heels, is governed by other and more urgent considerations."

Mantatisi did not expect this attack, which came in the winter of 1822. Her people were scattered all over her territory and her army was partially demobilised. She quickly realised their situation was hopeless and, after some bloody skirmishes, gave the order for her people to gather their cattle and whatever other possessions they had and take flight.

Mpangazitha and his warriors finished off the old and sick people the Batlokoa had to leave behind and harvested the crops that remained in the fields. But they had to hurry, because the amaNgwane were right behind them.

Mantatisi and her people initially sought safety and shelter with her brother Letlala, chief of the Basia. Letlala wanted her to stay so that they could fight Mpangazitha together, but Mantatisi feared that her own people might start fighting with the Basia. She probably also realised that after Mpangazitha came Matiwane, so staying on the move would be best. The chief of another Batlokoa clan, Nkgahle, also offered his alliance, but Mantatisi didn't trust him.

Soon after Mantatisi had left, Letlala and Nkgahle's people were dislodged by Mpangazitha and also started a life on the run. They both later asked to join Mantatisi. She would gather many other groups into her clan over the next few years.

Mantatisi fled westwards, first overpowering the Bafokeng clans, called the Mist People, living west of present-day Bethlehem. The chain reaction had begun: raiding, ransacking and running, a process that would be repeated over and over.

The Batlokoa lived in the Mist People's villages for a while but were again attacked by Mpangazitha. This time, Mantatisi was ready for battle and fared a lot better against the amaHlubi.

Mantatisi and her people remained on the move, this time across the Caledon River to the flat-topped mountain at Botha Bothe, in the north-west corner of what is today the kingdom of Lesotho. This was where a young chief of a branch of the insignificant clan of the Bamokoteli, Moshoeshoe, had settled his adherents after he split from his father, Mochachane, at his village at Menkhoaneng.

In about April 1823, the Batlokoa attacked Moshoeshoe. At one point, the Bamokoteli took on the Batlokoa warriors and drove them back to the camp where their women and children were waiting. A young Tlokoa woman, Maseile, grabbed one of Moshoeshoe's soldiers and shouted insults at him, which so fired up the Tlokoa men that they fought back and forced Moshoeshoe and his men to

flee the area. The encounter was known as *Ntoa-ea-Lipatsana*, the Battle of the Pots, because all the Batlokoa's clay pots were broken.

During the following spring, after Moshoeshoe had returned to Botha Bothe, Mantatisi and Sekonyela returned and laid siege to the mountain. Sekonyela had unwisely destroyed all the millet fields, so the Batlokoa were not much better off than the Bamokoteli on top of the mountain, who ended up eating all their dogs.

Moshoeshoe later found a new mountain fortress, Thaba Bosiu, where he established his capital and collected enough cattle and people to become the most powerful Sesotho-speaking chief ever – in fact, he became the founder and king of a new nation he called the Basotho.

The Batlokoa moved further westwards, parallel to the Caledon River, which today forms the border between South Africa and Lesotho. Mpangazitha was racing in the same direction, but along the northern bank of the river.

Mantatisi's warriors, with Sekonyela now one of the commanders, had become an efficient killing machine, devastating everything in their path. Her victims sought out others to overpower. A killing frenzy broke out in the entire Caledon Valley and beyond, with many smaller groups heading for the mountains at the first rumours that Mantatisi's Wild Cat warriors were on their way.

It was inevitable that Mantatisi and Mpangazitha would have a showdown over control of the fertile valley. In the region of Peka, near present-day Maseru, she sent Sekonyela and the Batlokoa warriors to launch a surprise attack on Mpangazitha. There wasn't much in the battle and both armies went their separate ways. On his way back, Sekonyela attacked a small group near Berea and captured all their cattle, because the Batlokoa were desperately hungry.

Mpangazitha then seized his chance to finish off the Batlokoa. He knew Sekonyela and the entire Batlokoa army were away and launched a full-on attack on the main Batlokoa settlement, where Mantatisi herself and all the women, children, older men and possessions were sitting ducks.

It was only the never-say-die attitude and genius of Mantatisi that saved the day. The source of this amazing story is Dr Ellenberger, so I'll let him tell it:

> When she saw the enemy approaching, she gathered all the women together, and formed them in ranks in front of the camp, and in front of them she placed such males as were left in camp.
>
> These, brandishing mats and hoes, presented, when viewed from a distance, the appearance of a strong force of warriors, which gave pause to Pakalita [Mpangazitha], who hoped to find the camp defenceless, and caused him to halt and make fresh plans.
>
> Meanwhile, Mantatisi had sent hot-foot to recall her son, who arrived unobserved while Pakalita was still cogitating. Without hesitation or a moment's delay, Sekonyela flung his whole strength upon Pakalita before the latter was well aware of his arrival, and inflicted a severe defeat.

Mantatisi took her people further north after this battle, forcing the Batloung of Chief Montso and the Bakoena of Chief Makhetha to join her. Next she fell upon the Mist People again, driving them across the Vaal River and capturing most of their cattle.

For months on end Mantatisi's Batlokoa, now widely known and feared as the Bamantatisi, or the Mantatees, criss-crossed central South Africa, raiding and killing as they went, in a desperate effort to avoid being devoured like so many other small clans at the time. Some of the groups they overpowered joined them, while others scattered and became the victims of lions, cannibals or starvation.

Far away from all this drama, at a mission station at Kuruman, the Reverend Robert Moffat started hearing stories about this one-eyed giantess. "It was said that a mighty woman, of the name Mantatee, was at the head of an invincible army, numerous as locusts, marching onward among the interior nations, carrying devastation and ruin

wherever she went; that she nourished the army with her own milk, sent out hornets before it, and, in one word, was laying the world desolate."

Rumour became fact. For a century and a half afterwards historians, some of them big names, repeated the story that in June 1823 Mantatisi had launched a massive attack on the Tswana people at Dithakong, on the edge of the Kalahari. Her forces were repelled by the warriors of Chief Makaba of the Bangwaketsi, with the help of the Griqua, and hundreds of Batlokoa were killed, said the reports.

But Mantatisi was never anywhere near the scene. As William F Lye pointed out so convincingly in a 1967 paper on the Lifaqane in the *Journal of African History*, the attackers were people dislodged by Mantatisi, Mpangazitha and Matiwane over a long period, who banded together and started their own raiding activities.

By 1823, Mantatisi and her son Sekonyela commanded one of three dominant forces in the region around the Caledon River valley, the others being Mpangazitha's amaHlubi and Moshoeshoe's Bamokoteli. Mpangazitha was eventually defeated and killed by Matiwane of the amaNgwane; he, in turn, was eventually forced out of the area by Shaka's forces.

In 1824, after Sekonyela had taken command of her forces, Mantatisi settled down at Marabeng, near Ficksburg. Whereas most of the Sotho-speaking clans in what we know today as the Free State and Lesotho had been wiped out, scattered, starved or forced to flee across the Vaal, her people had survived the most traumatic time in southern Africa's history.

Mantatisi competed with men, but this does not mean she tried to become a man herself. Occasionally, we get a glimpse of behaviour that is distinctly feminine. According to JC MacGregor in his 1905 work *Basotho Traditions*, on one occasion she "sent the fighting men to forage for grain for the children". Elizabeth Eldridge observes: "Providing food for children was the responsibility of women, and men, especially warriors in the field, often had access

to meat which was not necessarily shared with women, much less children. At a time when granaries were empty from drought and the traditional foraging and gathering activities of women and children put them in danger of kidnapping by outsiders, women and children were at risk of starvation. In no other place in the traditions is the welfare of children ever a consideration, suggesting that Manthatisi's concern reflected a sensitivity to the needs of the more vulnerable members of society which a man might have overlooked."

Sending proud male chauvinist warriors to collect food for children also indicates that her authority wasn't questioned. MacGregor writes that Mantatisi "used to sit in court with the men on the biggest stone in the circle, hear cases and discuss politics; and the policy of the tribe during her regency was conducted by her alone".

The French missionary Thomas Arbousset, who was stationed with Moshoeshoe, wrote that Mantatisi was "a woman of great intelligence" with "a regular countenance and an elegant figure". Other European visitors who saw her towards the end of her life said she became overweight, with one even alleging that she was a drunk. Tlokoa descendants ascribe this to prejudice and sexism on the side of Europeans who did not like or understand the indigenous African.

Missionaries and travellers who visited her reported that she had about twenty thousand followers, many of them Nguni-speaking former refugees, after she settled at Marabeng and that her jurisdiction stretched for many kilometres on both sides of the Caledon River. The only Basotho chief whose influence could challenge hers was Moshoeshoe himself.

In a paper comparing Moshoeshoe and Sekonyela in the *Journal of African History* in 1969, PB Sanders writes that the Batlokoa and Moshoeshoe's Basotho were "roughly equal in strength" by 1828. But this changed quickly with Moshoeshoe's successful cattle raids among the Tembu and his remarkable nation-building tactics.

Sekonyela, who settled on the nearby mountain of Joalaboholo,

was a huge disappointment to his mother. He was a cruel and sullen figure who was feared rather than loved by his people – and he apparently smoked far too much dagga.

Sekonyela did stupid things like stealing some of Dingane's cattle, which were then recovered by Voortrekker leader Piet Retief, as well as cattle belonging to the Korana people of Gert Taaibosch, who had guns and horses. The Batlokoa paid dearly for these indiscretions, and by 1840 Moshoeshoe's empire had completely eclipsed that of Sekonyela. Sekonyela eventually fled to the Cape Colony.

Moshoeshoe's children were also a huge disappointment. When I once asked an old Mosotho living near the base of Thaba Bosiu why both Moshoeshoe and Mantatisi's children were so different from their parents, he answered: "Because only small trees can grow where a big tree once stood."

We do not know exactly when Mantatisi died, but it must have been around 1835. She was buried on Joalaboholo outside Ficksburg, where some of her descendants still pay homage to her every year, because without her remarkable leadership they would not have existed.

In April 2006, the first of three German Type 209 submarines bought by the South African Navy arrived in Simon's Town and was named the SAS *Manthatisi*. Chief Lekunutu Mmota of the Batlokoa, a descendant of Mantatisi, attended the ceremony.

7

The Darkie Boer

EVERY NOW AND THEN, SOMETHING HAPPENS THAT proves graphically how mindless and nonsensical racial prejudice is. There can hardly be a more telling story to illustrate this than that of William Jordan, alias Willem Jordaan, founder of the tiny Boer republic of Upingtonia.

William was born to Patrick and Margaret Jordan in Cape Town in 1848 and, according to the Methodist Parish Records of Wynberg, was baptised as William Worthington the following year. Patrick was a British immigrant, but Margaret was a Cape Town girl and, according to some sources, the daughter of a slave woman.

William wasn't as pale as his father – during the apartheid years he would have been classified a "Cape Coloured".

His parents weren't well off and could give their son no more than a basic education. He didn't seem to need more. He had an unusual thirst for knowledge and read everything he could find. He had a special interest in medicine and some said he knew more of medical matters than some of the quacks at the Cape.

But William Jordan had a soul far too restless – and ambitious and adventurous – to be a doctor. He was only twenty-one when he left Cape Town, trekking north and settling at Rehoboth, just south of present-day Windhoek, in Namibia. Rehoboth was home to a group of people of mixed race who had trekked from the south and called themselves Basters.

Using Rehoboth as a base, Jordan travelled north into Ovamboland, Kavango, Damaraland, the Kaokoveld and deep into Angola,

hunting, trading and observing. Through reports he wrote for newspapers in Cape Town, he opened up these faraway parts to South Africans.

By the late 1870s, Jordan was one of the most successful traders in the region spanning the present-day Northern Cape, Namibia and Angola. He was a legendary hunter and with his charismatic and sympathetic personality had made friends all over the place, including among the Portuguese colonial authorities in Angola. It helped that he was fluent in Portuguese, French and Dutch/Afrikaans as well as his mother tongue, English.

At the age of thirty, Jordan was wealthy enough to start having very ambitious dreams of opening up the whole of the western subcontinent to trade, from the Cape all the way across the Gariep and Kunene rivers to Luanda, capital of Angola – a vision not unlike that of Cecil John Rhodes for the central regions of Africa.

But instability in central Namibia threatened to thwart Jordan's plans for trade between the Cape Colony and the areas north of the Gariep and the Kunene. The dominant Herero were constantly at war with the Nama from the south.

Jordan tried his hand at brokering peace between the two groups but eventually gave up, working instead on an idea for the war-torn areas of Namibia to be "civilised", if needs be by people from outside, by which he meant white people.

When Jordan met a group of white trekkers in northern Namibia in 1878, he thought he had found the people who could be settled alongside the Basters to form a buffer between the Herero and the Nama. The Basters and these trekkers spoke the same language – a creolised version of Dutch called Afrikaans.

The trekkers were participants in what became known as the Dorsland (Thirstland) Trek. To understand this rather bizarre chapter in our history, we have to go back a few years before 1878.

Around 1873, a number of Boer families in the Transvaal – or the Zuid-Afrikaansche Republiek (ZAR) – from especially the Rusten-

burg and Pretoria regions began talking about trekking again. I say "again" because the Great Trek from the Cape Colony to the interior had ended a mere thirty or so years earlier.

This was no single, strong movement with a leader or an ideology, but simply a group of people who thought they should leave the ZAR. Most of them belonged to the more orthodox of the two main Afrikaans churches, the Gereformeerde Kerk – the *Doppers*, as its members are still known – to which Paul Kruger, president of the ZAR after 1883, also belonged.

The best reports about the early stages of this movement were published in 1873 and 1874 in *De Maandbode*, the journal of the Gereformeerde Kerk's theological college at Burgersdorp.

According to *De Maandbode*, one of the reasons the people wanted to trek was unhappiness with TF Burgers, who became president of the ZAR in 1872. He was a former *dominee* (minister), but from the slightly less orthodox Nederduits Gereformeerde Kerk. He was seen as a liberal by some, especially after he instituted laws separating state and church and banning religious teaching in schools. Some fundamentalists called him the Antichrist.

De Maandbode also reported that the Boers were unhappy with steps and laws leading to "the complete liberation of non-white peoples". Throughout the trek, the danger of *gelykstelling* (making equal) between black and white was a constant fear.

Professor JP Jooste, author of the *Gedenkboek van die Dorslandtrek*, published in 1974, believed that there was another, possibly more important reason: the *trekgees* (nomadic spirit). He quotes Gert Alberts and GJS van der Merwe, leaders of the first group to trek, as saying: "We had a moving spirit in our hearts to trek. The reason for this desire to trek [*treklus*] is not easily understood. Trek was in our hearts and we ourselves could not understand why."

Jooste also makes the point that the movement could not be called an emigration, because the trekkers had no fixed destination in mind. Some vaguely mentioned place names like Zambezi,

Damaraland and Canaan. Others simply said they wanted to trek "northwards".

The clergyman whom the first Dorsland trekkers asked to look after their spiritual needs, Dominee Cachet, wrote a letter with "worrying questions" to the trek leaders. He was concerned that they said they were leaving because black people were being liberated, and asked them to explain what their attitude was towards slavery. He also wanted assurances that they were not going to occupy by force land that belonged to other people.

Gert Alberts, his family and some of his friends were so restless that they began trekking around Rustenburg in early 1874, moving closer and closer to the border with Bechuanaland (now Botswana). As time went on, more and more families moved.

In May 1874, the first wagons crossed into the British protectorate of Bechuanaland, starting a traumatic journey across deserts and through tropical areas that would cost many of the participants their lives. A second group crossed the border in July 1875 and a third in April 1877. Between five hundred and six hundred people took part in the Dorsland Trek.

William Jordan encountered the first Dorsland trekkers in the south-east of present-day Namibia in 1878. Most of them were in a terrible state and Jordan did what he could to nurse them back to health. They called him Willem Jordaan.

According to JM van Tonder in his book *Kerk in 'n Beter Land: Die Kerkverhaal van die Dorsland- en Angola Trekkers 1873–1937*, written from a Gereformeerde Kerk perspective, "He [Jordan] was genuinely interested in them and quickly won over their confidence. They viewed him as a suitable agent to negotiate on their behalf."

Jordan was not only interested in the mental and physical health of the travellers. He thought he had found the "buffer" between the Herero and the Nama that he was hoping for: the people who would "civilise" central Namibia and stabilise his trade route.

Jordan established a strong friendship with one of the Dorsland

Trek leaders, Pieter Botha, grandson of Great Trek leader Gert Maritz. Together they rode to Walvis Bay on the coast to purchase a large tract of land around Rehoboth, where the trekkers could settle. But in 1880, renewed hostilities between the Nama and the Herero forced them to abandon this plan.

Jordan knew southern Angola well and knew the Portuguese colonial representatives there would welcome white settlers from the south. Following the outbreak of hostilities, he led the group of trekkers over the Kunene River and helped them settle on the highlands of Humpata in the south-west of Angola.

It is quite remarkable that people so obsessed with race that they left their homes because blacks had too much freedom accepted a black man's leadership. In fact, the Dorsland trekkers were not only conservative, they were downright racist. They refused to allow their "coloured" Afrikaans-speaking servants, who had made the journey with them and whom they called *mak volk* (tame folk), to attend the same church in Humpata. They went even further, refusing their minister permission to preach to the black congregation. One church elder cited six Bible verses he believed dictated that a preacher serving a white congregation could not "serve the kaffirs" as well. When Dominee H Pasch refused to apply this extreme form of apartheid, the congregation split.

The South African families lived and farmed around Humpata for four years, but when Jordan visited them in August 1884, he discovered that the "trek spirit" had overcome them once again. They were also unhappy with the Portuguese who, they believed, wanted to convert them to Roman Catholicism. The trekkers' schools were inferior, but they refused to send their children to the Portuguese schools because these were also open to black children.

In December 1884, some thirty-six families crossed back over the Kunene River. Jordan came to their rescue once again and invited them to settle on a new piece of Rehoboth land he had bought, but the sale was eventually thwarted by the Nama chief, Swartbooi.

In April 1885, Jordan bought a huge tract of land, about fifty thousand square kilometres in extent, between present-day Grootfontein, Otavi and Etosha from the Ovambo chief, Kambonde, for a horse, a cask of brandy and twenty-five rifles. The sale was witnessed by the Finnish missionaries stationed at Ondangwa, Kambonde's kraal (and a century later, one of the main bases of the occupying South African Defence Force).

Jordan believed that his land had more than mere agricultural value. He saw it as having great strategic value, since it lay on the trade route between Walvis Bay and present-day Zimbabwe. He was soon punting the idea of a railway line between the port and what was then Rhodesia, which would run across his land.

Jordan showed the trekkers the deed of sale and invited them to stay and farm the land. Most of them decided to accept, but his old friend Pieter Botha insisted that they trek back to the Transvaal. It was the beginning of serious bad blood between Jordan and Botha.

The trekkers were enthusiastic about Jordan's proposed declaration of the land he had acquired as an independent republic. They also accepted his suggestion that it be called the Republic of Upingtonia, after Sir Thomas Upington, prime minister of the Cape Colony. This would ensure that the new republic had the support of both the premier and his administration, said Jordan.

In October 1885, all the families in the area were called to a meeting at Otjivandatjongue, now known as Grootfontein. A proper constitution was adopted by all present and the leaders were chosen: GD Prinsloo as president, CL Leen as government secretary, LM du Plessis as magistrate and DP Black as *veldkornet.* Jordan was to be the republic's minister of foreign affairs.

He was also the keynote speaker at the founding ceremony, telling the trekkers: "This is an historic occasion, because after all the years of wandering, those gathered here stand at the formal establishment of an own state. That has been the ideal all these years. For this reason, the Trek started at the Crocodile River almost ten years ago.

At first it was hoped that the ideal state would be found north of the Kunene on the Angolan highlands. Perhaps I should admit to my own part in that mistake today."

But the new republic soon proved too good to be true. Robert Lewis, a British trader acting as an agent for Cecil John Rhodes, declared the sale of the land illegal because he had previously bought the mineral rights from the Herero, who were the true owners of the land. The Herero chief, Kamaherero, then appointed Lewis as *his* agent, and also claimed ownership of the land.

Botha was growing increasingly jealous of Jordan's wealth and popularity among the trekkers. He started making his own private business deals with Lewis, who also felt threatened by Jordan. Botha not only accused Jordan of building a personal empire and using the Boer families as tools, but even of conniving with British interests in the region.

Matters between Jordan and Botha culminated in a full-on confrontation when Chief Kambonde asked Jordan to mobilise a commando to recover his stolen cattle from a group of Bushmen. Botha and some of his supporters confronted the Jordan commando, trying to force them back. Jordan called Botha a traitor; Botha said he didn't care what Jordan thought of him, because Jordan was not a white man.

This stung Jordan, because his skin colour had never been a factor in his relationship with the Boer families. After the incident, Jordan was reassured by the other citizens of Upingtonia that they were every bit as outraged at Botha's insult as he was himself.

Botha and Lewis lobbied Chief Kambonde to turn his back on Jordan, telling the chief that Jordan had tricked him. The Republic of Upingtonia was furthering the interests of his brother, Chief Nehale Mpingana, they told Kambonde. Lewis even threatened that he would start supporting Nehale, who had ambitions of becoming the leader of all the Ovambo people.

Jordan and the Upingtonians approached the German high

commissioner in Windhoek to mediate between themselves, the Herero and the Ovambo. The Germans were sympathetic and even sent an emissary to Upingtonia.

The Germans disliked the fact that the republic was named after a British colonial official, however, and Jordan and his fellow rulers declared that they would change the name of Upingtonia to the Republic of Lydensrust. Not even that, in the end, brought any action or protection from Germany.

Chief Kambonde eventually wrote a letter to Chief Kamaherero, denying that he had ever sold the land to Jordan, despite the fact that Finnish missionaries had witnessed the sale and co-signed the documents.

Jordan decided to visit Kambonde to sort matters out. On 30 June 1886, on his way to Kambonde, he decided to stay the night at Chief Nehale Mpingana's kraal. Early the next morning, while Jordan was washing himself next to his wagon, Nehale arrived and talked about selling him elephant tusks.

Then, without warning, Nehale took out his gun and shot Jordan in the head. Jordan died on the spot, right next to his wagon.

According to Alf Wannenburgh's *Forgotten Frontiersmen*, Nehale also shot Jordan's lead ox, "and man and beast were buried together, where their bones remain mingled to this day in an unmarked grave near Olukonda in Ovamboland".

In 2002, Chief Nehale Mpingana was formally honoured at a ceremony at the new Heroes Acre on the outskirts of Windhoek. Apart from fighting against the German colonial forces at Fort Namutoni in 1904, the chief was credited in the official programme "for the demise of the Republic of Upingtonia when … he killed William Worthington Jordan, leaving the Boer Trekkers without a leader. They quickly dispersed."

Jordan's death indeed heralded the end of the Republic of Upingtonia/Lydensrust because the citizens relied completely on his leadership. Within months some of the families had trekked back to Humpata, while others returned to Rustenburg.

By the 1930s, all the Dorsland trekkers were back in South Africa or Namibia. It was the most senseless, ill-fated and absurd trek in the history of Africa.

8

The Secret Scribe

PERHAPS THE EXPLANATION FOR THE READINESS WITH which the Dorsland trekkers accepted William Jordan lies in their inherent respect for someone better educated, even though he was black. For the Afrikaners who left the Cape Colony for the interior during the first part of the nineteenth century, education was a rare commodity.

A man named Jan Gerritze Bantjes was one of the exceptions. Not only was he a fully-fledged Voortrekker, he was also one of the Great Trek's most prominent resident intellectuals.

In fact, Bantjes was the author of one of Afrikanerdom's most sacred documents: the treaty between Zulu king Dingane and Voortrekker leader Piet Retief. Bantjes actually took part in the Battle of Blood River and later became clerk of the Natal Volksraad (People's Assembly).

And here's an even more astonishing fact: some Great Trek historians believe that it was Bantjes who taught Paul Kruger – later president of the Zuid-Afrikaansche Republiek (ZAR) and one of Afrikanerdom's greatest icons – to read and write.

But Jan Gerritze Bantjes was not a white man. Like William Jordan, he was the descendant of slaves.

Born on 8 July 1817 at Nieuwveld in the district of Graaff-Reinet, Bantjes was the third child of Bernhard Louis Bantjes and Isebella Johanna Swanepoel. Bernhard's grandfather, Jan Geert Bantjes, arrived at the Cape in 1755 and on 5 March 1758 married Hilletje Agnita Jacobs, the daughter of two slaves, Jan Jacobs van die Kaap and Agnietie Pieters van die Kaap.

Bantjes left the district of Beaufort with *veldkornet* Jacob de Clerq and some family members in December 1836 and joined the Great Trek at Thaba Nchu on New Year's Day 1837. The Voortrekkers' *dominee*, Erasmus Smit, wrote in his diary: "Mr De Klerk [De Clerq] has brought with him a young coloured man, and since the latter has some talents, I requested him to read a passage and to sing. He pleased me very much; his name is Jan Bantjes."

Dominee Smit's reference to Bantjes' race is the only one that I could find in historical records. In virtually every account of the Great Trek there is reference to Bantjes as the "secretary" or "scribe" or even "amanuensis" of, at different times, Voortrekker leaders Andries Pretorius, Piet Retief, Gert Maritz and Piet Uys, but never a mention of his race.

Such an omission might be considered entirely normal in the modern world, but in the nineteenth century South African society was obsessed with race. There were several hundred "coloured" people who made the Great Trek as retainers or servants, and they were most definitely treated as socially inferior.

In *The Voortrekkers*, his popular book on the Afrikaner exodus, Johannes Meintjes states that "Jan Gerritze Bantjes was to play an important role in Trek history as a schoolmaster and general recorder of the scene" but makes no mention of the fact that Bantjes was a black man. In *Forgotten Frontiersmen*, Alf Wannenburgh says the writing skill of Bantjes "was such that within a short time he appears to have been able to write himself white in their eyes".

While Bantjes was serving with Uys, he drew up the report on "Natalland" which caused the Uys group to trek to Natal to join Piet Retief's group. There is general consensus among historians that Bantjes was the author of the treaty between Retief and Dingane, in terms of which the Zulu king gave the land between the Umzimvubu and Tugela rivers to Retief.

The document, in Bantjes' handwriting and signed on 4 December 1838, read:

> Know all men by this that Whereas Pieter Retief, Governor of the Dutch Emigrate South Africans has retaken my cattle which Sikonyela had stolen which cattle he the said Retief now deliver unto me, Dingaan King of the Zoolas as hereby certify and declare that I thought fit to resign unto him the said Retief and his countrymen (on reward of the case hereby mentioned) the place called Port Natal together with all the land that is to say from Dogellato the Omsoboebo river westwards from the Sea to the north as far as the Land may be useful and in my possession which I did by this and give unto them for their Everlasting Property.

Two days later, Retief and some of his men went to Dingane's kraal, umGungundlovu, to bid the king farewell. Dingane had them all clubbed to death, an incident that remained etched in the memory of Afrikaners for more than a century afterwards.

It was Bantjes, at this time secretary to Andries Pretorius, commander of the *Wenkommando* against the Zulu, who carried news of the Retief party's terrible demise to the main body of Voortrekkers.

The most sacred events in all of Afrikaner history are the covenant made at Waschbankspruit on 9 December 1838, when the Voortrekkers vowed that if God granted them victory over the Zulu forces, they would forever honour the day as a sabbath, and the actual Battle of Blood River a week later. Bantjes took part in both, and his account of these momentous events, published in a special edition of the Cape journal *De Zuid-Afrikaan*, is the seminal document on which historians have relied ever since.

In 1839, Bantjes was appointed clerk of the Volksraad of the Republic of Natal and also started appearing as a lawyer in the Pietermaritzburg court. But when the widow HJ van Niekerk sued him for a substantial amount of money he had borrowed from her, he went back to the Cape to escape the court case.

Bantjes next popped up at Humansdorp in the Eastern Cape, where he served as a schoolmaster and reader in the Nederduits

Gereformeerde Kerk. He also ran a shop in Prince Albert for some years. In 1855 he left for Graaff-Reinet, and in 1863 he moved to Pretoria, where he became the magistrate's clerk and, later in the same year, the postmaster of the ZAR. By the end of his life, Bantjes had also served as a criminal prosecutor and school principal in Lichtenburg and Ventersdorp.

Jan Gerritze Bantjes died in 1887 at his eldest son's home in Potchefstroom. A year earlier his younger son, also called Jan Gerritze, had become the first gold miner on the Witwatersrand.

9

Cutting Off the Head of the Tortoise

THANKFULLY, THE SOUTHERN AFRICAN REGION HAS not been plagued by too many *coups d'état*. We had one in Lesotho in 1986 and a year later there was one in the apartheid bantustan of Transkei. Some would say the way Robert Mugabe "stole" the 2008 Zimbabwean elections also amounts to a coup. But that's about it.

Perhaps aspirant plotters in the region read their history and realised how badly wrong a coup could go. Because one of the most disastrous, even comical, attempts to overthrow a government happened in these parts in the first days of 1896.

After all, have you ever heard of an armed invasion of a country that saw soldiers send messages to their girlfriends in the territory to be invaded, telling them when they would be home? Where an officer on sick leave accompanied the invading force in a horse-drawn cart as a spectator who wanted "to see the fun"? Where special French champagne was shipped to the invading soldiers to get them into the right mood for the attack?

South Africa did not yet exist as a state in 1896. The region was made up of two British colonies – the Cape and Natal – and two Boer republics formed after the Great Trek: the Zuid-Afrikaansche Republiek, also known as Transvaal, and the Republic of the Orange Free State.

This is the story of the attempted overthrow of President Paul

Kruger's government in the ZAR by a motley group of British imperialists and gold-mine bosses.

It is a strange story. It would have been a funny story if not for the fact that this episode was a prelude to the war that broke out between the British Empire and the two Boer republics, which turned out to be the most vicious ever fought on the African continent.

The geopolitics of southern Africa changed fundamentally after rich diamond deposits were found at Kimberley in 1870, and the discovery of the world's richest gold deposits on the Witwatersrand in 1884. The city of Johannesburg was founded as a mining town in 1886 and, by 1895, foreigners from all over the world who came to seek their fortune outnumbered the white Afrikaans-speaking citizens.

The foreigners were called *uitlanders* by the Boers of the ZAR and were regarded with some hostility. Still, they were tolerated because they paid most of the republic's taxes and sustained almost the entire education system. In fact, the ZAR administration had become quite corrupt, with many civil servants and politicians unable to resist asking for bribes from the rich mining men.

In the minds of the Boers, these realities did not mean that the émigrés should have the vote or the right to have their children educated in any language other than that of the republic, namely Afrikaans. The very reason they were called uitlanders was because they were not citizens. President Kruger declared that the Afrikaners were so outnumbered that "if we give them [the foreigners] the franchise tomorrow, we may as well give up the republic".

The uitlanders, most of whom saw the Boers as a rather inferior, backward people, insisted on the same treatment – voting and language rights – as that of Afrikaners who had not taken part in the Great Trek to the north, but had remained under British rule in the Cape Colony.

It was this conflict of interest that the prime minister of the Cape, arch-imperialist and mining magnate Cecil John Rhodes, decided to exploit. He had big dreams of a united South Africa linked to

other colonies to the north, all sparkling jewels in the British Crown and, as importantly, under his control. The ZAR with all its gold was the shiniest of all these gems.

If the uitlanders couldn't vote Kruger and his men out of office and take over the gold-rich republic, why not remove them by force? Rhodes was fabulously rich, so financing an invasion and uprising wouldn't be a problem, and he was extremely well connected politically in Britain, where he knew his idea of getting rid of the Boers would receive quiet approval.

His plan was simple. Paint a stark picture of British subjects in Johannesburg being repressed by an evil regime, mobilise the uitlanders to revolt and see to it that there would be a friendly British force in the vicinity to protect British lives when the uprising began.

Naturally, the prime minister of the Cape Colony couldn't be seen to be planning an armed invasion into a neighbouring territory, so Rhodes turned to his old friend, a Scottish medical doctor named Leander Starr Jameson.

Doctor Jim, as he was widely known, suffered from short-man syndrome. He compensated for his lack of stature with a façade of machismo and confidence, even arrogance. Instead of healing people, he became a military adventurer. A few years earlier, Jameson had led a group of armed men and settlers across the Limpopo River and fought a war on behalf of Rhodes in what later became known as Rhodesia, now Zimbabwe. His title was administrator of Mashonaland.

Other men also played a role in the Rhodes invasion plan. Uitlander dissatisfaction gave rise to political rallies and the launching of protest bodies, and this resistance was galvanised when Charles Leonard, an attorney who shared the Cape premier's imperialistic visions, revived and invigorated the Transvaal National Union in 1892. The Reform Committee became the heart of the National Union and played an important part in the attempted coup.

We can trace the beginnings of the conspiracy back to December 1894, when Rhodes visited London. Jameson went with him, as did

the secretary of his Chartered Company, Dr Rutherfoord Harris. Rhodes was in London to lobby the prime minister, Lord Roseberry, and the Colonial Office.

Rhodes needed to acquire a base in British-ruled Bechuanaland (now Botswana) where the armed force could gather, and a high commissioner who wouldn't stand in his way. His choice fell on Sir Hercules Robinson – whom Kruger always referred to as "Sir Herklaas" – who was duly appointed.

On 4 December 1894, Queen Victoria wrote in her diary that Rhodes had said the Transvaal "which we ought never to have given up" would soon come under British rule once again.

Six months later, Britain found itself with a new prime minister, Lord Salisbury, and a new colonial secretary, Joseph Chamberlain. The powerful Chamberlain had his own imperialist dreams for southern Africa and knew he could achieve them only by working with Rhodes, the man known in London as the "uncrowned emperor" of the region.

British journalist and author William Stead met with Rhodes and wrote that his message in London was that it was an urgent priority to get rid of President Paul Kruger, who had "ten more years of mischief in him". Stead quoted Rhodes as saying, "We cannot wait until he disappears; South Africa is developing too rapidly. Something must be done to place the control of Transvaal in the hands of a more progressive ruler than Oom Paul."

Rhodes bought a chunk of land, about sixty-five square kilometres in extent, at Pitsani in Bechuanaland from two Tswana chiefs. The transfer was approved by Robinson and Chamberlain in October 1895. The staging area for the planned invasion was now secured.

Sir Hercules Robinson quickly appointed Leander Starr Jameson as "resident commissioner" of Pitsani and gave orders that the movement of the Chartered Company's troops from Mashonaland to Pitsani be facilitated – a sure indication that he already knew what Rhodes had in mind.

Next, Rhodes had to co-opt the big capitalists from the gold fields, the Randlords, who had thus far been fairly apolitical. He decided to use Alfred Beit, of the powerful Wernher-Beit-Eckstein group and a partner in the Goldfields group, as his point man. It was Beit's job to rope in his group's top executive and chairman of the Chamber of Mines, Lionel Phillips, as well as Charles Leonard of the National Union. With Jameson, these men formed the heart of the conspiracy.

Leonard wasn't a Randlord, but a committed British imperialist and jingo. He despised the Boers and once wrote that he did not believe in the "fiction of the Arcadian simplicity of the Boer". He told everyone who would listen that the Boers were unfit to rule any country and that the English-speakers in the ZAR would be satisfied with nothing less than control of the territory.

Late in October 1895, Rhodes convened a meeting of some of the main conspirators at his official residence, Groote Schuur. Among those present were Leonard, Phillips, distinguished American mining engineer John Hays Hammond and Colonel Frank Rhodes, Cecil's brother.

Rhodes sold his coup plan on the grounds that he merely wanted to assure democracy, full rights for uitlanders and good governance – "reform", as it was called. He told his guests, whom he wanted to execute his plans, that all he wanted in return was that the new rulers of the republic should facilitate free trade between the different states and colonies of South Africa.

Leonard, like so many other conspirators, was seduced by Rhodes. "I hesitated at first but was gradually drawn under by the singular magnetic power of Rhodes," he wrote long after the drama was over. On another occasion he wrote: "Step by step I was drawn further, and I can now see how skilfully my weaknesses – nay! My strength – were played upon – how I was *used* – until retract was all but impossible."

But Leonard maintained that he insisted on, and got, assurances from Rhodes that the independence of the ZAR would be maintained and that bloodshed would be avoided.

Colonial Secretary Chamberlain clearly also knew by this time that there were plans to muster an armed invasion force on the border of the ZAR – letters to him by Earl Grey, director of the Chartered Company and a friend of both Chamberlain and Rhodes, confirm this beyond doubt.

With the launch pad in place and the invasion force organised, the internal part of the plot now had to be attended to. The plan was to stir up an uprising among the uitlanders, which would then necessitate intervention by a friendly force to protect the rebels – Jameson's force at Pitsani.

In Johannesburg, Charles Leonard, Lionel Phillips, Frank Rhodes and John Hays Hammond formed a secret committee to coordinate activities. They carefully selected a handful of men who were invited to join what later became known as the Johannesburg Reform Committee.

The Chartered Company paid a vast amount – around £200 000 – into two accounts on which Reform Committee leaders could draw to finance the uprising and invasion.

Jameson told his fellow conspirators that he would assemble about fifteen hundred men at Pitsani. He planned to bring the same number of extra rifles with his invasion force, while another five thousand rifles, one million rounds of ammunition and three Maxim artillery pieces would be smuggled to the rebels in Johannesburg. This was indeed done under the leadership of Gardner Williams, general manager of the De Beers Company in Kimberley.

If that wasn't enough to fight a real war, Jameson planned to attack the state arsenal in Pretoria and take ten thousand more rifles, a dozen artillery pieces and twelve million rounds of ammunition.

Jameson met the Reform Committee in Johannesburg on 19 November 1895 to finalise the plans. The Johannesburg uprising was scheduled for 28 December.

But Jameson (and Rhodes?) needed an insurance policy in case things went wrong. So on 20 November, he dictated a letter to

Leonard, in which the Reform Committee asked Jameson to come to the rescue of the uitlanders.

"The position of matters in this State has become so critical that we are assured that at no distant period there will be a conflict between the Government and the uitlander population," the letter stated. It then sketched the position of the uitlanders as "rapidly becoming intolerable". They paid virtually all taxes, yet had no representation and were increasingly feeling insecure. "Public feeling is in a condition of smouldering discontent," the letter read, adding:

> Not to go into detail, we may say that the Government has called into existence all the elements necessary for armed conflict. The one desire of the people here is for fair play, the maintenance of their independence, and the preservation of those public liberties without which life is not worth having. The government denies these things and violates the national sense of the Englishmen at every turn.
>
> What we have to consider is, what will be the condition of things here in the event of conflict?
>
> Thousands of unarmed men, women and children of our race will be at the mercy of well-armed Boers; while property of enormous value will be in the greatest peril. We cannot contemplate the future without the gravest apprehension, and feel that we are justified in taking any steps to prevent the shedding of blood, and to ensure the protection of our rights.
>
> It is under these circumstances that we feel constrained to call upon you to come to our aid should disturbance arise here.
>
> The circumstances are so extreme that we cannot avoid this step and we cannot believe that you, and the men under you, will not fail to come to the rescue of people who would be so situated. We guarantee any expense that may reasonably be incurred by you in helping us, and ask you to believe that nothing but the sternest necessity has prompted this appeal.

The letter was signed by Charles Leonard, Frank Rhodes, John Hays Hammond, Lionel Phillips and mining magnate George Farrar, prominent leader of the British community in Johannesburg. Leonard realised how vulnerable the letter made the signatories and, the next day, asked for his signature to be removed. Jameson laughed and said the letter had already been sent to Rhodes in Cape Town.

The invasion force was ready and the plot began to unfold. Phillips started stirring the pot on the very evening that the letter to Jameson was signed. All the top mining and business officials were invited to the opening of the new Chamber of Mines building. Phillips delivered a rousing speech and a vitriolic attack on the government of Paul Kruger.

The English-speakers outnumbered the Boers three to one but paid nine-tenths of the state's revenue, he said. Conditions in the ZAR were deteriorating fast and the government was getting worse by the day. All efforts to negotiate with Kruger's regime were in vain.

"Nothing is further from my heart than a desire to see an upheaval, which would be disastrous from every point of view, and would probably end in the most horrible of possible endings, in bloodshed," Phillips said. "But I would say that it is a mistake to imagine that this much maligned community which consists anyhow of a majority of men born of freemen, will consent indefinitely to remain subordinate to the minority in this country, and that they will forever allow their lives, their property, and their liberty to be subject to its arbitrary will."

The speech was the signal for the games to begin. The Johannesburg daily, the *Star*, took up the campaign against the Kruger government – its editor, FH Hamilton, was a member of the Reform Committee. The newspaper went as far as saying that "the political death of Mr Kruger is absolutely indispensable to the dawn of the better day".

The Reform Committee started sending a stream of cables to British newspapers, outlining the ills of the Kruger government

and the impending uprising, and the newspapers lapped it up. *The Times* declared that the Kruger government was "the last refuge of patriarchal despotism" whose end was nigh. Denys Rhoodie, in his book *Conspirators of Conflict*, quotes the *Standard and Digger's News* about these cables: "The Tory press has tumbled to them with readiness, and from their tone one might almost imagine that the whole thing had been prearranged, that they were waiting instructions from this side to open fire, to perfect the anti-Boer Campaign, to damage and damn the reputation of the Boer and his Republic in the eyes of the great English Nation."

The newspaper concluded: "Indeed, between cable messages and the criticisms, we have evidence almost strong enough to suggest conspiracy."

But the plans for the "spontaneous" uprising were not proceeding according to expectation. Not one of the leaders of the Reform Committee was a true revolutionary or a mobiliser of people.

More seriously, Leonard and Phillips began to realise that Rhodes and Jameson had not been honest about their real agenda. They were not truly concerned with the interests of the English-speakers in Johannesburg. Rather, they wanted to expand Rhodes's own empire.

The secret committee members also discovered that Rhodes was lying to them about preserving the integrity of the ZAR. He – and Chamberlain in London – simply wanted to colonise the Boer republic. Their plan was for the invasion to take place under the Union Jack.

There were other reasons, too, why the plot started collapsing. The smuggling of arms into Johannesburg was taking place at the pace of a trickle; the men who had to capture the state arsenal reported that too many Boers would be in Pretoria around Christmas to take holy communion; several senior Randlords – men such as Barney Barnato, Sammy Marks and JB Robinson – couldn't be persuaded to take part.

But, most importantly, the ordinary men of Johannesburg who

had to stage the actual uprising that would trigger the invasion had no intention of doing so. As Captain Francis Younghusband of the Reform Committee wrote to *The Times* in London: "The old saying that Englishmen are never so peacefully employed as when they are engaged in making money is fully borne out here at the present time. Rebellion and money-making do not go together."

From early December, the telegraph lines between Johannesburg and Pitsani, Pitsani and Cape Town and Johannesburg and Cape Town began to sing. Jameson's raid was referred to as "the flotation" or "the polo tournament" and Jameson himself was called "the veterinary surgeon".

Jameson made it abundantly clear that any delays would be disastrous and that he wasn't prepared to wait beyond the end of December. The closer it got to the end of the month, though, the more hesitant the Johannesburg leg of the conspiracy became.

On 26 December, Charles Leonard issued a manifesto containing the Reform Committee's ten demands of government, stating that if there wasn't a positive response, the uitlanders of Johannesburg would rise up on 6 January 1896.

On the same day that the ultimatum was issued, the Johannesburg leaders sent urgent messages to Rhodes in Cape Town to order Jameson to postpone the "flotation". Telegrams were also sent directly to Jameson to tell him to stay put.

On 27 December, the Cape politician John Xavier Merriman wrote to Leonard regarding his manifesto. "You must be prepared for action after such very decided talk and you must also be prepared for a good many of the weaker brethren falling away. I confess that I did think that the agitation was only the squealing of capital under the knife of the tax gatherer. And for that there is no hope but there is a ring about your address which looks like business. Can you move the well-to-do working man? Until you do, the Boer will beat you. Revolutions are not made by those who live soft, but require a backbone of men who have corns on their hands."

Not surprisingly, President Paul Kruger's government knew by now that something was about to happen – possibly even knew details of the whole conspiracy. On 26 December, Kruger warned during a speech at Bronkhorstspruit: "I'm often asked about a threatened rising, and I say: wait until the time comes. Take the tortoise; if you want to kill it you must wait until it puts out its head; then you can cut it off."

Kruger nevertheless rushed back to Pretoria and, the following day, told the Reuters news agency that he was aware of the seriousness of the situation in Johannesburg and that it would be dealt with in time. The commandant-general of the republic was told to hurry back to Pretoria and additional men were sent to reinforce the mounted police in Johannesburg.

Christmas had seen panic starting to build up among the inhabitants of Johannesburg. Thousands of women and children began to flee the city. There were riots at the Braamfontein and Park stations as thousands tried to secure seats on trains out of town. Prices of commodities increased sharply, businessmen hired armed guards to protect their premises and some shops were boarded up.

The American writer Mark Twain (real name Samuel Langhorne Clemens), who toured South Africa during this time, described the episode thus: "As soon as it was known in Johannesburg that Jameson was on his way to rescue the women and children, the grateful people put the women and children on a train and rushed them for Australia. In fact, the approach of Johannesburg's saviour created panic and consternation there, and a multitude of males of peaceable disposition swept to the trains like a sandstorm. The early ones fared best; they secured the seats – by sitting on them – eight hours before the train was due to leave."

Rumours were rampant in the City of Gold. Groups of people gathered all over town, desperate for more information about the roots of the imminent unrest. It was widely speculated that some or other organisation was about to declare war on the ZAR government, but nobody knew what this organisation was.

Leonard and Hamilton told Rhodes by telegram late on Saturday 28 December that they were "absolutely unprepared for a revolution". The following morning they informed the other Johannesburg conspirators that Rhodes had asked Jameson to postpone his invasion – he had even said he could keep Jameson's force on the border for several months while conditions for a revolt were being fomented.

The Johannesburg leaders also sent two emissaries, Major Maurice Heany and Captain Harry Holden, to Pitsani to make sure Jameson got the message. Holden went on horseback and arrived first, but his arrival merely egged Jameson on. Heany, an old friend of Jameson's, took a special train from Kimberley to Mafeking, where he bought a horse. He arrived the morning after Holden.

Heany met Jameson in his tent, where he took out his notebook and read the message from the Johannesburg conspirators asking for a delayed departure of the invasion force. "Jameson rather laughed," British historian Elizabeth Longford (the Countess of Longford, CBE) reports in her book *Jameson's Raid*. "He and his lads, he promised, would kick the burghers all round Transvaal." (Famous last words, as they say in the classics.)

Holden and Heany then joined Jameson's raiding party. They were not the only late additions to Doctor Jim's force – a Major Crosse, who was on sick leave from the police, rode with them in civilian clothes and in a cart he provided himself. He wanted to go along just for the fun. When the other fighting men were tried and punished after the raid, he was found to have been "only a spectator" and let go.

Who could blame Major Crosse for thinking this was going to be a great adventure? The enemy wasn't to be feared, the end destination offered many diversions and, at Pitsani, the alcohol flowed like water.

Doctor Jim had a weakness for black velvet, the drink Rhodes had introduced him to: champagne mixed with stout. But he was a sharing leader: he had thirty-six cases of champagne brought to Pitsani for Christmas and gave his men permission to be "drunk for

three days" in preparation for the raid. Quoting Wilfred Blunt's *My Diaries 1888–1900*, Elizabeth Longford says that one of the raiders called the whole adventure "a regular drunken frolic". The *Cape Times* wrote in a commentary on the raid, "It would indeed have been dramatic irony if the gallant invaders of the Transvaal had needed Dutch courage."

On Sunday 29 December 1895, Jameson sent a telegram to Dr Henry Wolf, an American, fellow doctor and also a friend of Rhodes, to cut the telegraph wires. Wolf was also tasked with preparing stop-overs and provisions for the invading force along the route to Johannesburg.

The telegraph wires were indeed cut, but another roundabout line via Zeerust – through which the raiders had to pass – and Rustenburg was still operational. One of the troops responsible for cutting the wires was apparently so drunk that he botched the job – he cut a wire fence instead ... It was a telegram sent through this line that would inform General Piet Joubert of the ZAR armed forces that the raiding party had crossed into the Transvaal.

Jameson also sent the following telegram to the leaders of the Reform Committee: "Shall leave tonight for the Transvaal. We are simply going in to protect everybody while they change the present dishonest government and take vote from the whole country as to form of government required by the whole." The Johannesburg conspirators, by now desperate to stop the invasion, were not too alarmed, because they believed he must have sent his telegram before receiving the cable from Rhodes ordering a postponement.

During these tense days, it was the intention of Rhodes to withdraw to Groote Schuur and remain incommunicado. He informed the imperial secretary at Cape Town, Sir Graham Bower, of the Jameson invasion only on the evening of 29 December.

On that Sunday afternoon, the trumpets called the men to the Pitsani square. There were three hundred and fifty-six of them, with about one hundred and fifty more to join later at Mafeking.

It wasn't as simple as a mere send-off. Some of the men had serious doubts about the legality and wisdom of the mission; others, the champagne now out of their systems, were not in a fighting mood. But Jameson couldn't afford to have any of them drop out – he had promised the other conspirators more than seven hundred men, and was already two hundred short. So he had to talk even the most reluctant riders into joining the column, and joining enthusiastically.

Jameson began by reading the letter he had dictated to Charles Leonard and which was signed by the conspirators in Johannesburg – it became known as the "women and children" letter.

"Thousands of unarmed men, women and children of our race will be at the mercy of well-armed Boers, while property of enormous value will be in the greatest peril," Jameson read. "We cannot contemplate the future without the gravest apprehension, and feel that we are justified in taking any steps to prevent the shedding of blood, and to ensure the protection of our rights. It is under these circumstances that we feel constrained to call upon you to come to our aid should disturbance arise here." Why, only a coward could have refused such a plea for help.

Jameson called his planned raid an historic event and a crusade, saying if all went well there would be no bloodshed. He promised each man a special bonus and then played his last card: this act would be in service of Her Majesty the Queen.

It worked. The men cheered and sang "God Save the Queen" with great passion. Then they rode out with rations for one day only, because they would be catered for along the way.

The two groups of men met at Malmani (Ottoshoop), about sixty kilometres from Pitsani, very early on the Monday morning. By the time they had breakfasted, a full description of the number of raiders, their weapons and their location had been telegraphed by one Marais, the commissioner of mines at Ottoshoop, to the government in Pretoria.

The distance between Pitsani and Johannesburg is about two hundred and ninety kilometres. Henry Wolf and his men had erected five corrugated-iron sheds at various intervals along the planned route. These contained bully beef, biscuits and feed for the horses. Wolf's cover was that he operated the "Rand Produce and Trading Syndicate" and not even his own employees knew the true purpose of these refreshment stations.

Wolf also bought several hundred horses to replace the raiders' tired mounts and kept them on a farm, which the invading force reached on the second day. The horses and the food stations cost him £18 000, which came from one of the funds set up by Rhodes.

But when the party arrived at the farm, they could not catch the horses in time and discovered that, in any event, most of them were not suitable for riding long distances. So the men stuck to the horses on which they had left Pitsani.

From this point on, many important people tried their level best to get Jameson to stop in his tracks or go back to Pitsani. General Joubert telegraphed Commandant JDL Botha via the unbroken line and told him to cut off the raiding party. Botha then sent a telegram to Jameson, which was given to him when he arrived at McArthur's Stores, warning him that he would be stopped by force if he didn't turn back.

Jameson telegraphed in turn that he intended to proceed with his original plans, because he was invited by the "principal residents of the Rand" to secure their human rights. He signed his telegram, "Yours faithfully, LS Jameson".

There was no way Jameson could have thought that Botha wasn't serious. From the second day onwards his column of men was continuously flanked by small contingents of armed Boers on horseback. I suppose he was still convinced that he and his lads would kick the burghers all round Transvaal.

The next urgent order to abandon the plan came from Sir Hercules Robinson and was taken to the raiding party by an officer

who rode all the way from Mafeking. Jameson at first refused to open the envelope containing the message, and when he eventually did, he decided to ignore it and not even to respond. Turning back was not an option for Doctor Jim.

Robinson's warning was probably prompted by a message he had received from the colonial secretary, Joseph Chamberlain, who was informed on 29 December that Jameson's party had crossed the border into the Transvaal. Chamberlain even threatened to cancel Rhodes's Chartered Company concessions if the raid went ahead.

The *veldkornet* of Krugersdorp, JC Bodenstein, told the *Standard and Digger's News* that he had heard of a young woman whose fiancé, a member of the Bechuanaland Border Police based at Pitsani, had written her a letter saying he would be reunited with her around New Year. He would not be alone, he told his sweetheart – his entire armed force was planning to be in Johannesburg at that time.

John Fisher quotes Bodenstein in *Paul Kruger: His Life and Times* as saying: "On hearing the confirmation of the report in the letter, I went at once to Pretoria. I got there at eleven o'clock at night, and early the next morning I met the resident and informed him about the letter and about what I had been told. He remarked quietly, 'Yes, I have heard all about it.' General Joubert then added: 'All right: I will send you the necessary ammunition.'"

The Reform Committee held an emergency meeting on the night of Monday 30 December. They knew they could not denounce Jameson, because he was carrying their letter begging him to come and help. But they also realised that campaigning for the vote and other rights was a lot different than supporting an armed invasion under a foreign flag, so they swore allegiance to the ZAR and hoisted the ZAR flag, the Vierkleur, over the Goldfields building.

Then the committee sent a telegram to Robinson, the British high commissioner, stating that Jameson's action had put Johannesburg in peril and urging him to go to the city to mediate and prevent a full-scale war.

The Reform Committee wasn't backing down all the way, though. The following day – the last of the year – they issued a statement declaring themselves the Provisional Government of Johannesburg. In hindsight, it appears clear that they were keeping the door open just in case Jameson's invasion was successful.

At the same time, the committee prepared for a possible government attack. Subcommittees were formed with tasks ranging from medical services to police patrols of the city and "control of natives". Trenches and artillery positions were dug and arms and ammunition distributed. Shops, bars and mines were closed, windows boarded up. A Bicycle Club and a Ladies' Revolver Club were formed – and on the first day of target practice, the club's instructor, Sir Drummond Dunbar, lost his finger in a shooting accident.

Meanwhile, the Kruger government had sent Eugène Marais, famous author and at the time editor of the newspaper *Land en Volk*, and Abraham Malan, son-in-law of General Joubert, to Johannesburg on Monday 30 December to assess the situation. They reported that they had been told the uitlander resistance could consist of up to forty-five thousand men and that there were twenty-four Maxim guns and eight Nordenfeldt cannon in the city. (Someone put a huge iron pipe on a wagon, covered it with a tarpaulin and towed it through the city streets to start the rumour that the Johannesburgers had a huge cannon …)

The next day, Marais and Malan asked for a meeting with the Reform Committee and addressed them in the Goldfields building. They warned that while the old president would not hesitate to crush any armed resistance, he was prepared to listen to arguments for concessions. Lionel Phillips and three others then met with Chief Justice Kotzé, Judge HA Ameshoff and Jan de Kock, representing the ZAR government.

Phillips told the government delegation that if Jameson were allowed to reach Johannesburg unhindered, they would guarantee his immediate peaceful departure from the ZAR. "We come, as it

were, with the rifle in one hand and friendship in the other. If the hand of friendship is accepted, we will say, take our guns, we trust you."

Phillips was tricked into handing over a list of sixty-two names of members of the Reform Committee to prove that the committee was indeed speaking on behalf of the uitlanders of Johannesburg.

At the end of the meeting, Chief Justice Kotzé told the Reform Committee delegation that the ZAR government had accepted an offer from Sir Hercules Robinson to go to Pretoria to help prevent bloodshed. Until his arrival, the government would not act against anyone in Johannesburg – on condition that the Johannesburgers took no action either. This arrangement didn't include Jameson, who was regarded as "a foreign invader", Kotzé said.

On Wednesday 1 January 1896, another messenger on horseback reached the advancing Jameson column. He carried a message from Sir Jacobus de Wet, British agent in Pretoria, on the orders of Chamberlain himself: "Her Majesty's Government entirely disapprove your conduct in invading Transvaal with armed force; your action has been repudiated. You are ordered to retire at once from the country and will be held personally responsible for the consequences for your unauthorised and most improper proceeding."

Jameson responded that he had peaceful intentions and had thus far "not molested anyone". He maintained that he had made a promise to his countrymen in distress in Johannesburg, and he intended keeping it.

In reality, Jameson could not go back. His men and their horses were dead tired and there were no provisions or fresh horses on the way to Pitsani. They were barely fifty kilometres outside Johannesburg and it made no sense to him to turn back now.

Jameson also received various messages from the Reform Committee, some delivered by dispatch riders on horseback, others by men on bicycles. He later said one of the messages promised that a force of a few hundred men would await him in Krugersdorp; the Reform Committee denied ever saying anything of the kind.

The Boer commandos that had been shadowing the raiding party for days now laid a perfect ambush for Jameson in a deep valley outside Krugersdorp. Just west of the town, an advance guard ran into a commando, which then disappeared like mist before the sun. Jameson's senior officer, Sir John Willoughby (like his friend, Jameson, a man of very short stature), sent a message to the Boer commander threatening to shell Krugersdorp unless his party was allowed through. He did not even get a reply.

When Jameson looked down into the valley, he could see that he was going to have to fight his way through or surrender. Willoughby then indeed fired away at the Boer positions with his big guns, but to no effect. He ordered his men to storm the ridge where the commandos were entrenched. The Boer marksmen picked them off one by one. Within an hour, Willoughby had lost sixty men – dead, wounded or captured.

"Sir Johnny", whose horse Harvester won major races in Britain at the time, was said to have taught the young Winston Churchill the art of war, using toy soldiers. But his leading role in the Jameson Raid showed he wasn't much of a military genius.

When the commandos blocked his way and eliminated so many of his men, he decided to go around Krugersdorp. He found a guide to show him the route, but unfortunately the guide was a Boer supporter, who led Willoughby's men straight into enemy lines. Willoughby later claimed the treacherous guide was an agent of the Reform Committee, which wanted him to fail.

By nightfall on New Year's Day, Leander Starr Jameson knew he was in deep trouble, and if his friends in Johannesburg weren't going to send reinforcements as he expected them to do, he would have to consider defeat. He dispatched a messenger to Johannesburg with a note that read, "The Doctor is all right, but he says now he would like some men sent out to meet him."

The reply that his comrades in Johannesburg sent back was a proclamation from the British high commissioner, forbidding

British citizens from assisting Jameson. Around eight o'clock on 2 January, Jameson also received the Reform Committee's statement that they intended to obey the proclamation. Dr Jim was now an outlaw.

Early that morning, Willoughby had led the worn-out force along another road that he thought would be a short cut to Johannesburg. In fact, the route took the invaders directly to the Boer commandos' final ambush. The hapless Sir Johnny had selected yet another Boer sympathiser as his guide.

The Boers were waiting for Jameson's party on and around a hill called Doornkop. Jameson's reinforcements never materialised, but artillery support for the Boers did, and was firmly in place.

After a short exchange of shells, the Jameson party raised a white flag – in fact, it wasn't a flag at all, but the rather unclean white apron of one of the servants. Seventeen of Jameson's men were dead, thirty-five were missing and fifty-five were wounded. As the flag of surrender went up, Boer soldiers appeared from all over "like ants", one officer said. Most of them wore ordinary working clothes, but some were still dressed in the suits they had put on for the New Year church service.

This was how Willoughby described the decision to lay down arms: "Surrounded on all sides by the Boers, men and horses wearied out, outnumbered by at least six to one, our friends having failed to keep their promises to meet us, and my force reduced numerically by one fourth, I no longer considered that I was justified in sacrificing any more of the lives of the men under me."

A traumatised Jameson walked up to the Boer commanders, Piet Cronjé, Abraham Malan and Hendrik Potgieter, and formally surrendered by handing over his sword. Cronjé later said Jameson was "trembling like a reed".

The Boers treated the wounded Britons and buried their dead before taking Jameson and all his officers to jail in Pretoria. Two weeks later, President Paul Kruger handed the men over to the British

government on the border of Natal, after which they were shipped to London.

For a long time afterwards the favourite joke among the Afrikaners of the Transvaal was to ask, "What colour is the British flag?" When the answer came, "Red, white and blue", the questioner declared, "Wrong. I have seen it twice, at Majuba and at Doornkop. It is a dirty white rag." (A strong British force was defeated by the Boers at Majuba in February 1888.)

In England, the dishonourable end to Jameson's adventure was viewed with gloom – and anger at the folly of it all. But this lasted one day only.

On 3 January, the German emperor, Kaiser Wilhelm, sent the following telegram to President Kruger. (Apart from being the emperor of Germany, Wilhelm – or William – was also Queen Victoria's grandson and an admiral in the Royal Navy.)

> Berlin. 3 January 1896.
> I express to you my sincere congratulations that without calling on the aid of friendly powers you and your people by your own energy against the armed bands which have broken into your country as disturbers of the peace have succeeded in re-establishing peace and defending the independence of the country against attacks from without.

Historian Elizabeth Longford describes the reaction to the telegram thus: "In little more than fifty words the Kaiser managed to do what no British statesman could have hoped to achieve after ten times the effort. He rallied the whole nation. What was more, he created an uproar in which Jameson was either deified or forgotten … an abashed jingoism found its voice again."

Queen Victoria sent her grandson a "My Dear William" letter, gently rebuking him and saying his telegram was "considered very unfriendly to this country" and made "the most unfortunate impression" in England. To which the Kaiser replied:

> Most beloved Grandmamma, Never was the Telegram intended as a step against England or your government. I thought the raiders were a mixed mob of gold-diggers … the scum of all nations, never suspecting that there were real Englishmen or Officers among them. I was standing up for law, order and obedience to a Sovereign whom I revere and adore.

The French government congratulated President Kruger by presenting him with a ceremonial sword, adorned with the figure of a Boer throttling the imperial lion.

In reality, Kruger emerged from the whole debacle as the victor. He had not overreacted to Jameson's aggression; he had not been provoked into acting violently against the uitlanders in Johannesburg; he had resisted pressure to hang Jameson and instead handed him to the British authorities.

Sixty-four members of the Reform Committee were arrested and charged with treason. The four ringleaders were sentenced to death and the rest to two years in prison and a hefty fine each. But in the end, all the accused received clemency and got off with a fine.

Kruger submitted a claim for £1 000 000 for "moral and intellectual damage" and another for £677 983, plus three shillings and three pence, for the cost of suppressing the uprising. He declared, "If a poor man's dog comes into my garden, I shoot it. If a rich man's dog comes, I tie it up and make his master pay."

The biggest loser after the Jameson Raid wasn't Jameson – he returned to South Africa and, less than ten years after the incursion, became the prime minister of the Cape. Cecil John Rhodes was the man who lost the most. Although Chamberlain defended him in the British parliament and although Rhodes never faced any direct sanction, it was no secret that he was behind the fiasco. He eventually resigned as prime minister.

Paul Kruger blamed Rhodes for the whole affair and insisted that Chamberlain "knew all about the matter". Kruger stated in his

autobiography, *The Memoirs of Paul Kruger*, "Rhodes had long entertained the project of making himself master of the Republic in one way or another; and he devoted his money, his influence and his position as Premier of the Cape Colony to this object."

Kruger made clear what he thought the significance of the Jameson Raid was when he referred to it immediately after the end of the Anglo-Boer War in 1902 as "the first act of the drama of which the last act has just been finished on the bloodstained plains of South Africa".

10

The Saga of Billy and Oom Koos

THE TWO MAIN CHARACTERS IN THIS STORY COULDN'T be more different. One was a staunch Calvinist, patriarch and war hero, the other a ruthless gangster, killer and robber. They never met, but for one of them, their connection was fatal.

Let me introduce you to the war hero. His name was Jacobus Hercules de la Rey, known to most as Koos and later as Oom (Uncle) Koos. Yes, it's the same De la Rey who made a comeback in 2006 in a popular Afrikaans song that stirred a great deal of controversy with its chorus, "*De la Rey, De la Rey, sal jy die Boere kom lei?*" (Will you come and lead the Boers?).

De la Rey was born in 1847 on a farm near Winburg in the Free State. His first military experience was fighting with the Free State Boers against the Basotho in 1865. As a young adult, he moved to the Lichtenburg district in the old Transvaal Republic and became a community leader and successful farmer, even though he had no formal education.

But it was as a general during the South African War of 1899–1902, also known as the Anglo-Boer War, that he made his name. He was initially reluctant to support President Paul Kruger's decision to wage war against the British Empire, eloquently urging Kruger during the last debate in the Volksraad to avoid conflict.

Kruger came close to accusing him of cowardice. De la Rey said he would abide by the decision of the Volksraad and, addressing

Kruger directly, he declared: "And you, you will see me fight in the field for our independence long after you and your party who fight a war with your mouths will have fled the country."

Those were prophetic words. Right up to his death fifteen years later, De la Rey would be the most powerful inspiration for Afrikaner nationalism. With his aquiline nose, flowing beard and piercing eyes, he was seen as a *volksvader* (patriarch of the people) and a leader sent by God himself. He was affectionately known as *Die Leeu van die Wes-Transvaal* – the Lion of the Western Transvaal.

Military analysts who have studied the Anglo-Boer War describe De la Rey as a brilliant strategist and one of the early experts in guerrilla warfare. He and General Christiaan de Wet were the Boer commanders most feared by the British army.

Even Lord Milner, who represented the ugliest face of British imperialism and despised the Boers with a passion, said of De la Rey after the war: "He is a remarkably fine fellow; he is a man, every inch of him; and one of whom any country in the world might justly feel proud."

But despite the bravery and cunning of the Boer soldiers, they lost the war. Part of the reason for the Boer loss was the scorched-earth policy applied by the British – burning Boer farms and killing cattle – and their concentration camps, where some 28 000 women and children died. These practices left deep scars on the Afrikaner psyche.

De la Rey was part of the leadership that negotiated the Peace of Vereeniging in 1902 and a member of a delegation that went to Europe shortly afterwards to raise funds for the upliftment of the Boer people. Then he went back to being a farmer outside Lichtenburg, but he stayed in touch with the old Boer prophet Nicolaas "Siener" (Seer) van Rensburg, who had often accompanied his troops during the war and served the general as an adviser.

Siener was famous for his predictions of future events. He had, indeed, foretold the Boer defeat, Britain's scorched-earth policy and

the use of concentration camps years before these things came to pass.

De la Rey was said to have consulted Siener on even his operational planning during the war. One of his biographers, Professor AWG Raath, says some of the Boer commandos threw all caution to the wind when Siener was with them. If he said that there weren't any British soldiers in the vicinity, they regarded it as a waste of energy to set guards at night. There were many stories of how Siener's predictions about British troop movements proved to be correct.

Siener was also an Afrikaner nationalist of the fundamentalist kind. He was embittered about the Boer defeat of 1902 and the formation of the Union of South Africa under the British Crown in 1910.

After Britain declared war on Germany on 4 August 1914, the British government asked the government of South Africa to invade German South West Africa, as Namibia was then known, and to seize the main radio station at Windhoek as well as the harbour towns of Swakopmund and Lüderitz.

Prime Minister General Louis Botha, supported by General Jan Smuts, was amenable to this request, but some of their ministers and top army commanders felt it would be outrageous to fight for Britain a mere twelve years after that country had tried to destroy the Boer nation. Despite this opposition, a good majority in the Union parliament decided that South Africa should enter the First World War against the Germans.

Meanwhile, old Siener had made a comeback and started having visions again. If the Afrikaners used this war to regain their independence, it would be a pushover, he told De la Rey.

News that a Boer rebellion was brewing alarmed General Botha, who invited De la Rey to a meeting with his cabinet and top government officials. De la Rey repeated Siener's prediction of an Afrikaner takeover of South Africa. Botha and Smuts never really took Siener

van Rensburg seriously and this time thought Oom Koos was losing his marbles. But they knew that Siener's visions had created ominous expectations among Afrikaners, especially in the Western Transvaal. They made De la Rey promise that he would not do anything rash.

At this point, let's turn the clock back a few months. On Saturday 11 July 1914, Siener van Rensburg arrived at De la Rey's farm, Elandsfontein, some ninety kilometres from his own. It was his first visit to De la Rey's home, and the old general knew it had to be a serious matter that brought the prophet there.

According to De la Rey's daughter Polly, Siener was in tears for most of the time he was there. He loved and hero-worshipped De la Rey, the only Boer leader who really took him seriously.

Siener said he saw a piece of white paper with the figures one and five hovering over Lichtenburg. He saw a train carrying De la Rey's wife, Nonnie, and their children. Oom Koos was also there, but without the hat that he almost always wore. The train stopped at many places and crowds of people came to see it. They were all weeping.

It was an elaborate vision. Siener saw the train arriving at Lichtenburg, where the flags were flying at half mast. He saw many flowers. He saw a commando on horseback arriving from Schweizer-Reneke, and many trains. Then Siener looked at Oom Koos and told him urgently: "Oom Koos, you must be careful."

It's not clear whether De la Rey understood that Siener was predicting his imminent death or, if he did realise this, whether or not he took it seriously. He must have known that Siener's vision of him without a hat meant that he wasn't alive. Popularly, however, the vision was soon interpreted as meaning that the numbers one and five seen by Siener meant that the Afrikaner was going to be liberated again, on the fifteenth day of a certain month.

De la Rey did not keep his promise to Botha and Smuts and changed none of his plans or behaviour. He clearly believed Siener and organised a mass meeting at Treurfontein, some thirty kilometres

outside Lichtenburg, to tell Afrikaners about his vision of victory for the Boers. The men wanted to saddle up immediately and ride into Pretoria to declare a new Boer republic. Along with his old comrades like Boer War generals Christiaan de Wet, Manie Maritz and Christiaan Beyers, De la Rey planned a coup.

He went ahead with the organisation of a huge *volksvergadering* (people's assembly) on 15 September at Potchefstroom, to discuss the First World War and the possibilities it offered for taking over the government. On the appointed day, he arrived by train in Johannesburg, where he was picked up by General Beyers. Together, the two set off by car for Potchefstroom.

General Koos de la Rey never made it to the meeting. His life was snuffed out en route by a bullet meant for the other man in this story: William Foster.

In 1914, Koos de la Rey was sixty-seven years old. Foster was twenty-eight, the same age as the city of Johannesburg, which was founded in 1886. He was the son of John, an Irishman from County Armagh in Northern Ireland, and Elizabeth Smith, an English girl whose grandparents were British settlers, brought to the Eastern Cape in 1820. The couple had six children, three boys and three girls.

The Fosters first lived in Griqualand East, where John was a builder, but moved to the City of Gold when William was fourteen. They lived in the suburb of Fairview, and young William went to Marist Brothers College.

A fair amount is known about William Foster, thanks to police documents, court records, newspaper reports of the time and books like Napier Devitt's *Celebrated South African Crimes* of 1941 and *The Foster Gang* of 1966 by advocate Henry May, QC, and Iain Hamilton, then editor of the *Spectator*.

William, called Billy by his family and some friends, was a quick-tempered and rebellious boy, but his parents and teachers thought that was due to his Irish blood rather than a delinquent streak. He was an outstanding soccer player and his younger brother Jimmy's hero.

William passed his matriculation examinations at age seventeen and got a job as an apprentice surveyor on a gold mine. He was a natty dresser and cut a dashing figure on his motorcycle. He found his job boring and took up photography, becoming a professional photographer on the mines after he qualified as a surveyor.

The young Foster's next bout of restlessness took him to then German-controlled South West Africa after he heard that diamonds had been found at the coast. It was a turning point in his life.

It is not known what he did or what happened to him in what later became Namibia, but two months after his arrival, the German mounted police found him and two other young men driving a pack of donkeys towards the southern border. He was dishevelled, sunburnt and very thin. He was sentenced to a month in jail for cattle theft and according to reports was treated badly by his jailers because of his hostile behaviour.

Instead of going home on being released, William went to Durban, where he found a job at the docks. His life was beginning to seriously unravel.

First he got involved in a dockside brawl with some sailors, and after railway property was damaged, he was sentenced to four weeks in jail or a £10 fine. He didn't have the money, but on the way to jail he escaped – only to be caught the next day, riding the train to Johannesburg without a ticket.

William was in jail for three and a half months, but soon after his release he was again caught illegally riding a freight train to Johannesburg. Shortly after regaining his freedom, he was caught stealing a kitbag and this time was jailed for six months.

During all this time his family thought he was still in Namibia, because he never gave the police his real name; he was either Smith or Johnston.

He finally returned home after fifteen months, of which he had spent more than twelve in jail. He got a job with a firm of commercial photographers and tried to straighten out his life.

One night, he was sent to the theatre to take photographs of the cast of *Splash Me* during rehearsal. His eye caught one of the prettiest young singer/dancers, Peggy Lyons, and he asked her if he could take extra pictures of her afterwards. She agreed, and the two fell in love.

It turned out that Lyons was her stage name. Her real surname was Korenico, and she was from London. When her theatre company returned to England, she stayed behind.

Peggy was described as "a good, modest and respectable girl with an exceedingly sweet nature". Soon after their first meeting, she agreed to marry William when she turned twenty-one. William was happy to wait, because he wanted to make enough money to give his bride a house and every comfort.

In 1911, he travelled to England on a grant from his employers, who wanted him to report back on the latest trends in photography. His own idea was to make a fortune and come back to claim his bride.

But things didn't go well for William in England, and he arrived back in Table Bay harbour early in 1913. He stayed in Cape Town, quite desperate to make good money before returning to his fiancée, who had by then celebrated her twenty-first birthday.

This was the mood Foster was in when he and Fred Adamson, his school friend who happened to be in Cape Town at the time, met John Maxwell, a Texan who worked for a circus. Known as Jack Maxim, or as Cowboy Jack to some, Maxwell's trick was throwing a revolver in the air, catching it and then shooting down a row of apples perched on bottles. The circus crowds loved him.

Maxwell was a drifter who had spent almost a year in jail for selling liquor to black people – "natives" were only allowed to drink their own traditional sorghum beer at the time. But he was sick of struggling on the few shillings he made working for the circus, and had a grand plan to rob a jewellery store. However, he needed a few partners.

To William Foster, this was the obvious way out of his cash crunch. The plan demanded an extra hand, and William said his brother Jimmy was just the man. He took the train to Johannesburg and told Peggy and his family that he was about to make good money, and would be back to marry Peggy.

Jimmy Foster joined his brother in Cape Town on 8 March 1913. With Adamson, they rented a large room at Ebenezer House, a boarding establishment in Hope Street, and started preparing for their big heist.

Eleven days later, William and Jimmy Foster and Fred Adamson walked down Longmarket Street, their faces darkened and wearing cloth caps and false moustaches. William opened the door of the city's biggest jewellery store, the American Swiss Watch Company, with a revolver in his hand. The two male employees meekly allowed the men to tie them up.

A few minutes later, the three men from Johannesburg walked out with virtually every item of value in the shop stuffed into two suitcases, plus £500 in cash from the till. John Maxwell was waiting for them in his car on the opposite side of the street. They sped off and Maxwell dropped them near the boarding house. Then, with the cash in his pocket, he drove to Johannesburg.

The robbery was well executed and they might have got away with it had it not been for Harry Bloom. He was a dandy and former actor who loved to hang out at Ebenezer House, entertaining the owner, Elizabeth Lee, her sister, Abigail Manuel, and permanent resident Janet Kay.

Bloom, probably slightly jealous of the young men around his favourite ladies, had been keeping an eye on the three boarders. When news of the daring jewellery heist reached him the day after it happened, he remembered noticing the Foster brothers and Adamson leaving that evening with two suitcases and coming back shortly afterwards, still carrying the suitcases.

When Elizabeth Lee told him that they had left early the next

morning and had given her a pair of cuff links made of Kruger sovereigns, Bloom made the connection. He had read that Kruger sovereign cuff links were among the jewels stolen from the American Swiss Watch Company.

Bloom went to the police with his suspicions and they informed him that the company owners had offered a reward of £500 for information. The fact that he gave them the tip-off before he knew about the reward cost him dearly later.

Bloom accompanied the cops to Ebenezer House, where Elizabeth Lee told them that her three boarders had left in the taxi of Mr John Gallias the morning after the robbery. Gallias took them to the railway station, where the baggage room clerk, a man called Herbert Sephton, remembered the three men and pointed out their luggage, which he still had in storage.

The policemen opened the suitcases and found the missing jewellery, false noses, beards and moustaches and an assortment of equipment usually used by burglars. Two policemen hid in the baggage room and arrested William Foster the next day when he came to collect the suitcases.

The police found a letter from Peggy in William's hotel room (she called him "Chummy") with the Fosters' home address. They arrested Jimmy and Fred Adamson in Johannesburg the next day.

Peggy went to Cape Town and found a daytime job as a waitress at Casey's Café in Hout Street and a night job as a model at the art school in Victoria Street. She visited William in the police cells every day.

William Foster and Peggy Korenico were married in the Roeland Street Jail on 15 May 1913 by special permission of the authorities.

The trial in the Cape High Court started on 22 May. The courtroom was packed every day and newspapers devoted many columns to reporting on the proceedings and the characters in this drama.

At the end of it, the judge, Sir John Kotze, sentenced each of the three robbers to twelve years' imprisonment with hard labour.

Within days some ten thousand signatures had been collected in Cape Town and Johannesburg for a petition to have the sentences reduced. The minister of justice refused. The Foster brothers and Adamson began serving their sentences at Pretoria Central Prison.

The reward of £500 became a bone of contention that had to be settled in the High Court. Harry Bloom, Elizabeth Lee and Abigail Manuel, John Gallias and Herbert Sephton all claimed the money, now reduced to £450 because not all the stolen loot was recovered.

Bloom's case was clearly the strongest. Without his tip-off, the police would probably not have solved the case at all. Lee and Manuel believed that their information about the Kruger cuff links and their pointing out of taxi driver Gallias were crucial to solving the case. Gallias's argument was that he was the one who took them to the station, and Sephton claimed his memory of the suitcases solved the case.

In his judgment, Mr Justice Hopley said it was clear that the first person to give information about the crime should get the reward. That person was Bloom, and his information was crucial: "But for Bloom, it is quite likely that the criminals might have escaped altogether, for there is nothing to show that anyone else had sufficient knowledge or suspicion or had formed any theory which could have been communicated to the police," the judge pointed out.

However, this was not a question of charitable benevolence, but rather of a contract, said Judge Hopley. The American Swiss Watch Company had made an offer to the public, and persons with information who knew about this offer had entered a legal contract when they provided clues about the crime.

The judge concluded: "Bloom gave the right information and the first information; but is he entitled to the reward? He would be if he knew of the advertisement and of the offered reward at the time he gave the information. But he did not have that knowledge."

He would have loved to give Bloom the £450, the judge said,

but he had no choice other than ruling that "no contract was ever concluded between him and the defendants". Bloom appealed this decision, but the Appeal Court agreed with Judge Hopley.

Harry Bloom never visited Ebenezer House again.

John Maxwell, alias Jack Maxim, was never caught for the robbery and his accomplices never betrayed him. But he joined them in Pretoria Central in June that year anyway, having been caught, yet again, for selling liquor to black people.

Maxwell's release date was March 1914. William Foster swore that he would get out of jail before his Texan friend. From later developments, it appears that Foster and Maxwell spent their time together in jail making ambitious plans for a profitable criminal career. Their intention, as Foster later explained, was to make a vast amount of money quickly, spring Jimmy and Adamson from prison, take Peggy and drive in Maxim's big car to Mozambique, from where they could travel to Europe by ship.

William did get out before Maxwell. He got the prisoners working as tailors to make him a brown suit and buried it (or had it buried) with a pair of wire-cutters near the barbed wire fence around the stone quarry where the convicts worked every day.

On 27 February 1914, his brother Jimmy and their partner in crime, Fred Adamson, started a fight with other prisoners while working in the quarry. The guards all rushed over to stop the fighting, and William quickly cut the fence with his wire-cutters, put on his brown suit and disappeared.

It is not known where Foster went after his escape, but we do know that he met up with Maxim when he was released from prison a few weeks later. They were now ready to launch their plans for quick money and flight from South Africa.

Foster, Maxim and their new partner, a Dutchman called Carl Mezar (aka George Smit) set up shop at The Factory, a building notorious for its criminal inhabitants in Ferreirastown, on the edge of Johannesburg's present-day central business district.

Their crime spree started at the end of April 1914 when they robbed the Roodepoort post office and, shortly afterwards, the Vrededorp post office. In July they hit the National Bank in Boksburg North, where they shot and killed a man.

Two weeks later the police put up wanted posters for Foster, Maxim and Mezar with a £500 reward. No sooner were the posters up than the three bandits robbed the National Bank in Cleveland and then the biggest liquor depot in Jeppestown.

The Factory was no longer a safe haven and the trio found a new hideout at a cave in Kensington. It was a substantial cave, enlarged by gold prospectors years before, in which William and Jimmy had played during their childhood.

After a while, the three gangsters moved to an abandoned cottage in Regent's Park, where there was space to park Maxim's big American car, an Overland with the registration number TJ 1021.

Peggy, who had given birth to a daughter while William was in jail, often came to see him and spend the night at this house, and later moved into the cottage permanently.

William's plan was to get rich quick, spring Jimmy from jail and then drive with his wife and partners to Mozambique, where they would seek passage on a ship bound for Europe.

On 13 September 1914, the gang was robbing the Imperial Bottle Store in Fairview when they were interrupted by the police. They shot and killed two police sergeants and then got away.

By now, the "Foster Gang" was the most notorious group of criminals in the Union and dominated the front pages of newspapers. It was after the Fairview shootings that a woman who lived near the Regent's Park cottage saw their photographs on the front page of the *Star*. She realised that the three men she had seen on several occasions could be the Foster Gang, and went to the police to report her suspicions.

On 15 September, Detective Charles Mynott, Detective Layde, Detective Rory McLennan – a school friend of William's who was

married to his sister – and Constable Murphy went to the cottage that the woman had pointed out.

They sneaked into the house and saw the men outside in the yard. Peggy was sitting on the back seat of Maxim's car, her husband on the running board. Mezar was leaning against the bonnet, playing a mouth organ, while Maxim was lying under the car. McLennan identified William Foster before he was sent outside by Mynott to cut the men off if they tried to make a run for it.

Mynott then stepped into the yard with his pistol raised in front of him. "Hands up!" he shouted.

William reacted coolly, asking Mynott his name and denying that he was, in fact, the notorious William Foster. While he was talking, Maxim slowly passed him a pistol from under the car. Foster shot Mynott in the chest.

The gangsters jumped into the car and roared off, the other three policemen firing furiously at the moving vehicle. They got away, but one of the shots hit William in the arm.

Near the Primrose cemetery, the Overland hit a rock in the road and the axle broke. The car came to a standstill in a ditch. William sent Peggy and the baby to take a bus to the house where she had been staying. Then he, Maxim and Mezar made their way on foot to the cave on Kensington Ridge, just a few kilometres away.

On the same afternoon, Gerald Grace, a medical doctor and former mayor of Springs, drove to the Johannesburg General Hospital with his wife. They were going to visit their son, who had recently undergone surgery. Early that evening, Dr Grace was driving back to the Springs hospital in his big black car and in quite a hurry, because he was scheduled to assist at an operation.

Not too far from where Maxim's black Overland had veered off the main road near the Simmer and Jack gold mine, two policemen who were looking for the Foster Gang saw Dr Grace's black car and motioned for him to stop.

Dr Grace probably didn't even see the men, and simply sped on.

The policemen, sure that the vehicle was carrying William Foster and his friends, shot at the car, and it came to a halt. Mrs Grace was hit in the arm, her husband in the chest. He died at the scene.

The day before, on 14 September 1914, the South African parliament had voted overwhelmingly in support of Britain's request to invade South West Africa and attack the German forces. General Koos de la Rey had clearly stated his opposition to the decision in the Senate, then travelled by train to Johannesburg to meet with General Christiaan Beyers, who had just resigned as the Commandant General of the Union Defence Force in protest against the government's decision.

On 15 September, Beyers's orderly, Trooper James Wagner, drove the general's big dark Daimler through the streets of Johannesburg. His passengers were De la Rey and Beyers, who were on their way to Potchefstroom to prepare for a rebellion against the government of Louis Botha.

Beyers told Wagner not to take the direct route through the city, but to go through Orange Grove and proceed via Parktown, Vrededorp, Fordsburg and Langlaagte.

By this time, the entire Johannesburg police force was on the streets looking for the Foster Gang. The two generals went through their first roadblock in Orange Grove, but, on the orders of De la Rey, didn't stop.

De la Rey had no idea that the police were looking for the Foster Gang and thought the roadblocks had been set up to stop him and Beyers from reaching Potchefstroom. In fact, just before the start of their journey, Wagner had seen a policeman taking down the registration number of Beyers's Daimler.

In Fordsburg, Wagner again ignored police warnings to stop. At 9.15 that evening, the Daimler approached another roadblock, in Langlaagte. Two policemen, named Drury and Ives, were standing in the road with loaded rifles, bayonets fixed.

Ives waved at the car and shouted that it should stop. His order

was ignored, and as the car drove past him, he stabbed a tyre with his bayonet. Behind him, Drury also waved the car down and shouted, "Halt!" He thrust his bayonet into the car's headlights as it drove past him, which means the car couldn't have been travelling very fast.

Drury fired a shot at the vehicle. The bullet bounced off the street surface, hitting De la Rey in the back. It lodged in his heart and he died instantly.

Beyers was devastated. On the advice of the police, he drove the car to the nearby Fountains Hotel and had De la Rey's body carried into the only available room – room fifteen. Beyers phoned his friends and colleagues and told them of De la Rey's death.

Only when the commander of the local police came to meet him did Beyers hear that the roadblocks were aimed not at them, but at the Foster Gang.

De la Rey's body was taken to the Johannesburg General Hospital for a post mortem. For most of the night and the next day, distraught friends and family guarded his body.

At some point on 16 September, the famous sculptor Anton van Wouw arrived and made a death mask of De la Rey's face, apparently as a cast for the remarkably realistic bronze statue of the general that he made. After Van Wouw's death, the mask was auctioned and bought by a friend of the Van Wouw family. This man gave the mask to Professor Andries Raath of Free State University while he was writing a biography of De la Rey in 2007, called *De la Rey: 'n Stryd vir Vryheid*.

The reappearance of the mask in 2008 created a sensation, especially after Dr Munro Marx of Unistel Medical Laboratories tested beard hairs stuck in the mask for DNA and matched them to blood taken from De la Rey's great-grandson, Jacques.

Koos de la Rey was buried at Lichtenburg on the Sunday after he died. The funeral procession was exactly as Siener van Rensburg had described in his vision: the train carrying De la Rey's wife and

children and Oom Koos without a hat; the people lining the route, dressed in black and weeping; the flags flying at half mast; the commando arriving from Schweizer-Reneke.

On that same Wednesday, 16 September, after workers reported seeing three dishevelled men going into the Kensington cave, six policemen arrived at the mouth of the hideout, which can still be seen on the ridge above this suburb in eastern Johannesburg.

The first policeman who entered the cave with a torch was shot at. He fired a number of shots in return and called for reinforcements. The police then rolled boulders in front of the entrance to the cave.

Word of the Foster Gang's last stand spread quickly. The Johannesburg transport department capitalised on the event and ran special streetcars to Kensington. By mid-morning on Thursday 17 September, a huge crowd had gathered.

The three desperadoes in the cave decided they weren't going to be taken alive. They started writing suicide notes on cigarette boxes and scraps of paper found in the cave.

Writing these letters probably gave them comfort, because William wrote four of them to his wife, one to his sister and one to his mother. "My darling wife Peggy," started one. "Goodbye forever more, my darling. I loved you in life and I love you in death. We are all dying by our own hands, my darling. Please give my dear little baby to my poor mother and forgive me for this terrible blow and wrong I have caused you. I only regret, my dearest, that you are not here to say goodbye. Please warn Jimmy against this evil. Give my dying regards to Dad, Mother, sisters and brothers, especially to my dear, kind sister, Aggie. May God rest my soul in peace. Goodbye, goodbye, forever more. May we meet in a better world, dearest. I would like to be buried near my darling sister, Maggie. Kiss my little baby girl goodbye. Yours in Death, Chummy."

In another note he wrote: "May you forgive me for taking my life. I have no fear of death and, although I have been shot three

times, I will never surrender. Max and Boy [Mezar] will die with me, brave to the last. Kiss my baby. Goodbye from me and don't grieve for me."

The shortest note read: "Peggy, my darling, may God protect you. I would rather you kill yourself as I have than suffer as I have. May we meet in Heaven, darling little wife. Goodbye, goodbye. Husband Chummy."

Carl Mezar addressed a note to his "mates", saying: "May you think kindly of me. I hope you will grieve much for me. May we meet in a better world. Carl Mezar. Only a brave boy."

Mezar wanted to shoot himself after he completed his note, but couldn't. Maxim then shot him in the head.

The police had decided to try to persuade the gang to surrender. Detective George Martin went to the mouth of the cave to talk to William Foster. William asked that Peggy be brought to him and promised to surrender once he had seen her. He gave the address where she was staying in Germiston and asked for water and cigarettes. He even apologised to Martin for killing the policeman earlier.

At two o'clock that afternoon, the crowd of onlookers saw Peggy Foster, baby in arms, walk into the cave. A little later, William requested that his parents and sisters also be allowed to enter the cave.

The family conference went on for about two hours. William talked about his arrest in Namibia and his other experiences, again expressing regret that the gang had to shoot policemen. He was particularly bitter about Judge Kotze's verdict and sentence and the fact that the petition with ten thousand signatures had been of no effect.

Peggy begged William to allow her to stay and die with him. She was going to kill herself anyway after he was dead, she said.

At about five o'clock that afternoon, William's parents and sisters Agnes and Cecilia, carrying his baby daughter, emerged from the

cave. Ten minutes later, the police heard three shots. When they went into the cave, they found the dead bodies of Peggy and William Foster and Jack Maxim next to that of Carl Mezar.

The reign of the Foster Gang was over.

Koos de la Rey's rebellion had no less an inglorious ending. Some eleven thousand men, led by Boer generals Christiaan Beyers, Christiaan de Wet, Manie Maritz and Jan Kemp, did rise up against the government in October, but their rebellion was quickly crushed. Beyers drowned in the Vaal River trying to escape, while De Wet was captured and sent to jail.

11

The Uppity Wanderer

GENERAL KOOS DE LA REY WAS A MAN OF GREAT STATURE, respected as a war hero even outside the Boer circles from whence he came. So great was the reverence in which he was held that it quite possibly eclipsed his remarkable wife, Nonnie, who never received much attention as a special person during her lifetime.

Well, perhaps that's not entirely true. British officers who fought against her husband during the Anglo-Boer War had the highest regard for her. General Lord PS Methuen in particular treated her with great respect, even admiration – and she once took him a roast chicken.

Nonnie de la Rey belies the oft-promoted image of Boer women as illiterate and subservient producers of babies, and slaves to their spouses. She was clever, assertive and brave – qualities she needed when she fled from the British forces and lived like a gypsy for eighteen months.

Jacoba Elizabeth Greeff was born on 28 May 1856. Her father was Hendrik Adriaan Greeff, a wagon-maker, originally from a farm near Cape Town. Her mother, Suzanna Maria Redelinghuys, was the daughter of a nomadic farmer. Her parents were married in Hopetown in 1855.

Known as Nonnie (which translates as "Missy") from the time she was a baby, she was born while her parents were visiting family and friends at Tulbagh in the Cape Colony. She was only three months old when her life of trekking with her restless father began with a trip by ox wagon through the Free State to the Gariep River, which took them to Potchefstroom, in what was then called the Western Transvaal. Two years later, the family moved on to Marico, where they eventually settled for a while.

At one point during their long journey, the Greeffs ran out of water completely. With the children crying with thirst and the adults feeling weak and dehydrated, Hendrik Greeff went down on his knees and promised God that if He gave them water there and then, he would return to this very spot on his fiftieth birthday to give thanks.

Greeff told his minister, Dominee JC de Vries, that God told him to look for water in a nearby tree. At first he thought he was hallucinating, because how could there be water in a tree? But when he went to the tree, he found water that had accumulated in a cavity where the white stinkwood's branches forked. There was enough water for the family to drink and to take with them to their next stop, where the precious liquid was in ample supply.

True to his word, when he turned fifty in 1878, Greeff returned to the site of the tree, taking Dominee De Vries and many of his friends and family along to thank God for saving his family's lives. And when she turned fifty in 1906, Nonnie took her husband, children, friends and family back to the same white stinkwood tree to give thanks again, as did her daughter, Polly de la Rey, on her fiftieth birthday in 1937.

This gesture says a lot about Nonnie Greeff's character. Like most other Afrikaner pioneer farmers in the interior at the time, the Greeffs saw the Old Testament – or at least their strict Calvinist interpretation of the Christian Bible – as their guide to everyday living. Nonnie's father was the unquestioned patriarch and, even more so than her mother, the guardian of the family's morality and lifestyle. Her mother's primary role was defined as that of a loving, supportive wife and a caring, hard-working mother.

They read from the Bible and prayed first thing in the morning; they prayed before and after every meal; and they read from the Bible and prayed again every evening. God's hand was seen in everything that happened to them and they believed that being in Africa and "taming" the land were what God wanted them to do.

But, as we will see later, it wasn't really that simple. Nonnie's mother was actually quite a strong-willed person who owned her own property and conducted business for her own account. Like many Afrikaner – and black – women from traditional, patriarchal backgrounds, Suzanna Greeff (and later Nonnie herself) often pretended to be the quiet, obedient wife and servant, while actually being as much a leader of the family as the husband, or perhaps even more so.

It wasn't long before Hendrik's wanderlust interrupted the quiet life led by the Greeffs on their farm Elandsfontein and he took them on a six-month hunting expedition. By this time, Nonnie was old enough to help with the careful planning and packing of the wagon that would be their home for the entire period; the experience stood her in good stead later in life.

In 1867, having spent just enough time on their second farm, Doornfontein, to build a proper house, the Greeffs packed their wagon once more and set off on yet another adventure. This time, the family trekked all the way through the desert to Damaraland in the north-western corner of present-day Namibia. While living at Doornfontein, Nonnie had gone to school for the first time, though only for about seven months, but the Damaraland hunting expedition was one of the most formative experiences of her young life.

The route the Greeffs followed brought them into contact with very few other human beings, but presented countless dangers such as lions, leopards, elephants, buffaloes, crocodiles, hippos and snakes. When they did encounter other people, they were Tswana, Bushmen (San), Nama, Damara or Herero, couldn't speak any Afrikaans or English and were often suspicious and hostile.

But the major threats to survival were lack of water and food. Several times, while on the brink of dying of thirst, the family was saved by Bushmen, who always knew where to find water in the desert. On one occasion, Hendrik again had to appeal to God to send them water, and within a few hours it began to rain.

In Damaraland, Nonnie's mother fell pregnant once more. Hendrik wanted to send her and the children to Cape Town from Walvis Bay by ship, intending to reunite with them later. However, when Suzanna flatly refused to leave her husband, a trip back to the Western Transvaal was hurriedly arranged.

Following one of the known routes would have taken too long, so Hendrik decided to navigate their trek by the stars. Even as the crow flies, the distance from Damaraland to their farms was more than a thousand kilometres. Along the way, they often had to clear a path through the bush for their wagon; at other times, the vehicle got stuck in deep sand for days.

The baby was born in November 1868, somewhere in present-day Botswana. Four months later, in March 1869, Hendrik and Suzanna Greeff and their five children arrived back at their farm. Life after that was a bit more normal for young Nonnie.

The children of Afrikaners who left the Cape for the northern interior from the beginning to the middle of the nineteenth century, as well as those who lived during the early years of the Boer republics, generally had very little or no formal education. Nonnie Greeff was no exception.

She had only seven months of formal schooling, but throughout her family's travels she was educated by her father. Mostly they studied the Bible, but Hendrik also taught his daughter basic numeracy and Afrikaner history. As Zelda Rowan, who wrote a thesis on Nonnie while at the University of Pretoria, observed, Nonnie's "knowledge of spelling and punctuation was minimal", but good enough to write down some of her memories on two sets of pages that became valuable historical documents.

When Nonnie was thirteen, an Irishman came to live with her family as the children's teacher. This was extremely beneficial, since by the time her father fired the teacher because of his excessive drinking, she could speak English. This came in very handy when she had to negotiate with British army commanders in later life.

Rowan mentions the fact that Jan Gerritze Bantjes, the dark-skinned Voortrekker scribe we learnt about in Chapter 8, came to live in Lichtenburg while the Greeffs were there and that he probably tutored Nonnie at some point. The town was proclaimed in 1873 on the Greeff farm Elandsfontein, and the family lived in the town for a while, before moving to a farm called Manana, eighteen kilometres away.

In June 1871, Nonnie Greeff was affirmed as a member of the Nederduitsch Hervormde Kerk's Potchefstroom congregation. This was referred to as the "*Boerematriek*".

Hendrik Greeff had become a prominent citizen of the district and also the leader of the local commando. When Nonnie was twenty-one years old, a *veldkornet* from the Schweizer-Reneke district who was already a military hero, Koos de la Rey, went to visit Commandant Greeff on his farm and stayed a few days.

The meeting between Koos and Nonnie appears to have been love at first sight. Connie Luyt writes in *Romances to Remember* that Nonnie's "hands were quivering" and that, on his way back to Marico, Koos "heard her name echoing in the galloping sound of his horse's hooves: Nonnie Greeff".

The two met again six months later in Kimberley. The Greeffs were staying with Suzanna's father and went to buy maize, but it is not known why Koos was there. On their way home, the Greeffs stayed with Koos's parents in the Wolmaransstad district. By then, Nonnie stated later, she knew he was worth her love and trust.

Koos clearly felt the same way and arrived at Manana a month later to ask for her hand in marriage. Suzanna refused to give her permission, apparently because Koos was too poor.

Like a *goeie Boeremeisie*, Nonnie didn't fight the decision and accepted that she wasn't going to be Koos's wife after all – someone else would surely come along, she remarked. But a while later, Koos had a passionate letter delivered to Nonnie at Manana, in which he reiterated his request to marry her. He must have made a convincing argument, because after reading the letter Suzanna agreed that her daughter could marry Koos de la Rey.

While they were preparing for the wedding ceremony, Koos was ordered by the government of the Zuid-Afrikaansche Republiek to lead a military expedition against the Bapedi chief Sekhukhune. But Koos had Nonnie on his mind and returned home before the end of the military campaign so that the wedding could go ahead as planned.

Koos and Nonnie were married on 24 October 1876 by Dominee Jan de Vries of the Zeerust congregation of the Hervormde Kerk. She was twenty-one and he was twenty-nine. They would be together until his death thirty-eight years later. Nonnie once described their union as a strong and clear stream of water.

Sir Percy Fitzpatrick, a leader among the uitlanders (dealt with in Chapter 9) and author of the famous *Jock of the Bushveld*, who later became a friend of the De la Reys, wrote in his *South African Memories* that he was surprised Nonnie had so little to say about Koos and their marriage in her autobiographical notes. "It seems to suggest for a moment that she did not understand or appreciate him, but looked upon him as a mere husband … nothing to make a fuss about – until one gradually realises that this was also his attitude to her and that, far from being disparagement and neglect, it was the very highest tribute, and evidence of the most genuine and unselfish trust and cooperation. He was attending to his job, she to hers. Their mutual confidence was magnificent. To both of them we can see it was the same, plain duty and no heroics."

Zelda Rowan's explanation is that Nonnie wrote her memoirs when the general was already a people's icon and that her writing was

aimed at people who already knew who Koos de la Rey was. She therefore wanted to confirm the image he projected and believed that how he conducted himself as a husband and father was irrelevant.

Nonnie and Koos lived with her parents for a month or so after their wedding because he did not have a farm or any sheep or cattle. Her father gave them a load of wheat as a present, which they ground and exchanged for sheep. That wasn't enough to start a farm, however, so they went to scrape, collect and sell salt from the salt pans. When they had bought enough livestock, they returned to Manana and established themselves on the six hundred hectares Hendrik Greeff had promised his daughter years before.

But Koos wasn't a full-time farmer for long. As the clouds of war began to gather over the Boer republic, he became more and more involved in government affairs – as a commando leader, as a surveyor of farms and as the Native Commissioner of Western Transvaal, negotiating with local chiefs.

This meant that Nonnie was in charge of the farm. They hired a white foreman for a while, but she thought he was lazy and useless and fired him. Her role as obedient wife and meek mother started blurring into what was seen at the time as man's work.

After Nonnie's father died in 1884 and her mother four years later, she and Koos moved to the Greeff family farm Elandsfontein. Koos was elected Lichtenburg's commandant in 1885 and its representative in the Transvaal House of Assembly in 1893, which meant Nonnie was responsible for the building of their huge house, dams and irrigation systems and for overseeing all agricultural activities.

But here's the other remarkable fact about Nonnie de la Rey: between 1878 and 1897, she gave birth to twelve children, seven girls and five boys. This means that she was pregnant for nine out of eighteen years. Two of her sons died before their first birthdays. After her mother's death, Nonnie also took care of her four younger siblings as well as two other children. She thus had sixteen children of various ages to feed and look after. According to J Meintjes in

De la Rey: Lion of the West, Koos left most of the child-rearing to Nonnie, especially when it came to discipline.

Then, in October 1899, war broke out between the two Boer republics and the British Empire. Koos de la Rey would play a key role in the war from the very beginning, and their two eldest sons, Adriaan (they called him Adaan) and Jacobus, were also part of the Boer fighting force.

From the outset Nonnie, desperately anxious about her family's safety, tried to stay in touch with her husband and sons and often travelled to where the commandos were stationed. Koos sent her telegrams reporting their good health whenever he could.

On 28 November 1899, Koos was hit in the shoulder by a piece of shrapnel during the Battle of Tweeriviere. He continued to fight, his son Adaan at his side. Late that same afternoon, a piece of shrapnel pierced Adaan's chest. He told his father he was dying.

Koos carried Adaan to Jacobsdal, about fourteen kilometres away, arriving early the next morning. An hour later, the youngster died in his father's arms.

On 29 November, the magistrate of Lichtenburg brought Nonnie a telegram from Koos which read: "Our beloved son Adriaan died in my arms of a bullet that hit him during a heavy battle. His body will be put to earth tomorrow here in Jacobsdal. However hard it is for us, it was God's decision."

Nonnie was absolutely devastated. She immediately rushed to the front and arrived at De la Rey's camp four days later. She went to Adaan's grave and fetched his clothes from the hospital. She stayed in an empty house near Magersfontein and saw her husband regularly, spending Christmas and New Year's Day with him. She left by train on 7 January when Koos was sent to Colesberg.

As the war raged on, it became clear to the British generals that Koos de la Rey was going to be a real thorn in their side. They knew that he occasionally sneaked back to his farm to be with his wife and children. The British decided to harass Nonnie and launch a campaign to capture Koos alive.

But if they thought Nonnie de la Rey was just another docile Boer woman, they made a serious mistake. Whenever she saw British soldiers on her farm misbehaving or attempting to take her horses or cattle, she marched right up to the commanding officer and had a verbal showdown. She did this with generals Archibald Hunter, CWH Douglas and Lord Methuen, and in each case the generals ordered their men to back down. Nonnie de la Rey was earning herself quite a reputation.

At one point during the early stages of the war, Nonnie heard that the British officers thought she and her family were quietly starving. It was true, but Nonnie didn't want to give the British the satisfaction of knowing they were correct, so she scraped together a little flour, baked two fresh loaves of bread and had them delivered to General Douglas.

Methuen seems to have had particular respect for Nonnie. In November 1900, he allowed her to persuade him to order his troops not to take her remaining horses from the farm. A while later, he even went to visit her to discuss his orders to burn down her house. What would she do if that happened, he wanted to know. He offered to leave one building standing for her family to live in, but she rejected this suggestion. Lord Methuen left, and never gave the order to burn down anything on the De la Rey farm.

Eventually, though, her position in Lichtenburg became intolerable, and when Methuen advised her to leave, she did so, albeit reluctantly.

On 1 December 1900, Nonnie de la Rey left Lichtenburg with an ox wagon full of provisions, clothes, chickens and children, as well as a few cows for milk and sheep for meat. The man who lived next door to her house in Lichtenburg, an Indian trader named Ajam Abed, was a friend of the family and gave her a good supply of sugar, coffee, rice, flour and medicine.

As she had done with her father three decades earlier, Nonnie de la Rey began a life of wandering. It only ended when the war did in May 1902.

The wagon wasn't big enough for Nonnie, all her children and three servants, so she pitched a tent next to it whenever she could. Often, as the British forces closed in, this had to be done in total darkness. Whenever she reached a farm where the British soldiers had not yet burned down all the buildings, she and her family stayed in a structure with a proper roof. On more than one occasion, they also stayed in caves.

When she regarded it as safe, Nonnie also spent short periods with families who were still on their farms. And when the course of war allowed, she travelled to De la Rey's camp and stayed with her husband for a few precious days.

Britain's scorched-earth policy meant there were very few sheep, cattle or poultry – or even unharvested crops – left on the abandoned farms. The cows Nonnie took with her became invaluable, because milk was often the only sustenance she could give the children. Her chickens, transported in wire cages and released whenever they stopped for a day or longer, were worth their weight in gold, but for the most part, *mieliepap* (maize porridge) was what they survived on.

Occasionally, Nonnie would build a veld oven in the ground and bake bread and rusks. When Lord Methuen was wounded in battle with her husband's forces in March 1902, she sent him a small bag of rusks. When coffee, the Boers' favourite beverage, ran low, she roasted pieces of sweet potato, ground them and added this to what little coffee remained. When they ran out of sugar, they used wild honey.

The clothing the De la Rey family left home with had to last and ended up being mended and patched many times over. When a soldier stole a Union Jack and the green cloth covering a snooker table from the Wolmaransstad hotel, she eagerly used the fabric to make new garments for her children. (One of Koos de la Rey's offspring sporting a dress made from the British flag must have been quite a sight.)

Nonnie extracted starch from green mealies and added saltpetre

scraped from the wall of a house near Schoonspruit to make her own soap, and she also made her own candles from fat and pieces of material.

Of course, Nonnie was by no means the only Boer woman living rough in the veld during the war; hundreds of them ended up travelling all over the old Transvaal and Free State after their farms were plundered and burnt to the ground. Sometimes, one or two of these women and their wagons joined forces with Nonnie and her family. The wife of Koos de la Rey's brother Jan, for instance, travelled with Nonnie on more than one occasion.

Despite her husband being a fighting general – and one desperately wanted by his enemy – and being constantly on the run, it seems that Nonnie and Koos always knew each other's movements. Once, a British officer brought her a telegram from Koos, wanting to know where she was ... We know of a few occasions when Koos sent a Boer soldier to warn Nonnie that she was in danger, and there are also records of Koos sending food to his family. Husband and wife tried to spend special days like Christmas and New Year together.

Meintjes, for example, reports that Koos and Nonnie planned a day together on 24 October 1902 – their twenty-fifth wedding anniversary. Koos dressed in his best suit that morning, but instead of spending a romantic day, his forces were attacked at Kleinfontein and suffered heavy losses. Koos fought the entire battle in his suit, discovering only at the end of the day that two of the buttons on his jacket had been shot off – or so the story goes.

Nonnie was afraid that she was going to be caught by the British and taken to one of the concentration camps, where so many women and children died. But on those occasions when she did run into enemy forces, they made no attempt to arrest her, and she showed no fear. On the contrary, she always confronted them assertively and was treated with great respect.

The last significant battle of the Anglo-Boer War happened at Tweebosch on 7 March 1902. It was one of Koos de la Rey's greatest

victories that left 68 British soldiers dead, 121 wounded and 872 taken prisoner, while only eight Boer soldiers died.

General Lord Methuen was among the wounded. He was captured when his horse was shot and fell on him, breaking one of the general's legs. De la Rey went to where he was lying and shook his hand, expressing regret that they had to meet under such circumstances. "Oh, it's the fortune of war," Methuen responded. He asked how Nonnie was doing, and tried to explain to De la Rey why Boer women were being sent to concentration camps, a policy he did not agree with.

After treatment by the Boer commando's doctor, Methuen was put in a tent to rest. Nonnie heard of the battle and that Methuen was captured, and rushed to Tweebosch, where she immediately went to Methuen's tent.

The general, she later recorded, apologised for causing her so much trouble. She jokingly remarked that she had been far too clever to be caught by Methuen's soldiers.

De la Rey thought Methuen's injuries were serious and sent him off to hospital in Krugersdorp in a horse-drawn carriage. Before he left, Nonnie slaughtered and cooked one of her prize chickens and gave it to Methuen with some rusks as *padkos*, food for the road. De la Rey sent a telegram to Methuen's wife with the news that he was wounded, but would recover.

Some of the Boer officers and burghers, influenced by their dominee, were very unhappy that their enemy was treated so kindly, and forced De la Rey to bring Methuen back to the camp. De la Rey's men caught up with Methuen about thirty kilometres from Krugersdorp and took him all the way back. On arrival De la Rey, supported by Nonnie, stood next to his wounded fellow officer and explained to his men why sending the general to receive proper medical care was the correct and Christian thing to do. This time, the burghers accepted his decision, and Methuen made the trip to the nearest hospital for the second time.

Nonnie's life in an ox wagon ended when the Boer republics and Britain signed a peace treaty on 31 May 1902. She went back to Elandsfontein and spent the next few years rebuilding the house and the farm.

Nonnie de la Rey died on 12 August 1923, nine years after her husband was shot by the police (described in Chapter 10).

12

Two Brits, One Aussie and a Pack of Ice

THERE'S NOTHING UNUSUAL ABOUT AN UNSOLVED CRIME in South Africa, nor is the link between diamonds and crime anything out of the ordinary. But when you throw "unsolved crime", "diamonds" and "Oppenheimer" into one sentence, most people will pay attention.

This is the unusual story of the brazen theft of one of the twentieth century's biggest and most precious private jewellery collections: that of Bridget, wife of mining mogul Harry Oppenheimer.

Another famous personality features in this tale: Dr Percy Yutar, the man whose claim to fame was that he was the prosecutor who had Nelson Mandela sent to Robben Island. But in this story, Yutar is not the brilliant prosecutor; rather, he is probably the biggest reason the theft case was never closed.

In a sense, the crime *was* solved. Three men who were intimately linked to the stolen jewellery were arrested. One turned state witness, the second was discharged before the trial started and the third was found not guilty. Apart from these three, no one was ever a suspect.

Almost half a century later, the theft remains a good whodunnit. At the time of writing, Mrs Oppenheimer, nowadays known as "the Queen Mum of South African horse racing", is still very much alive, so I suppose there will still be people who remember what a public spectacle the court case was and how the three suspects became celebrities overnight. It was reported that the circulation of one

Johannesburg newspaper jumped by some thirty thousand for the duration of the court proceedings.

It is from the ample newspaper clippings, court records and a 1956 book – *Drama in Diamonds: The Story of the Oppenheimer Jewel Theft*, by two reporters from the *Star* in Johannesburg, Dennis Craig and Brian Parkes – that we get the full story of this remarkable unsolved crime.

But first, a bit of background on the Oppenheimers, whose family name was southern Africa's most famous in an era before the likes of heart surgeon Chris Barnard and liberation icon Nelson Mandela emerged.

The story of this South African dynasty starts in 1880 with the birth in Friedberg, Germany, of Ernest Oppenheimer. He joined a firm of diamond brokers in London when he was sixteen years old, and in 1902, thirty-two years after the first diamond was discovered at Kimberley, his employers sent him to the new diamond fields. By this time the British arch-imperialist, Cecil John Rhodes, had already gained control of all the diamond operations in Kimberley, under the name De Beers Consolidated Mines Ltd.

In 1917, Ernest secured the backing of John Pierpont Morgan Jr, a top American banker, and formed the Anglo American Corporation to exploit the world's richest gold fields, the Witwatersrand. In 1919 he formed Consolidated Diamond Mines of South West Africa (now Namibia) and, soon after, acquired a controlling interest in De Beers. By 1940 he had a monopoly on diamond production, controlled much of the gold mining in South Africa and had vast mining interests in present-day Zambia, Namibia, Tanzania and Democratic Republic of Congo. He was knighted in 1921.

Ernest Oppenheimer's son, Harry Frederick, was born in Kimberley in 1908. In keeping with Jewish custom, he had his formal bar mitzvah at the Kimberley synagogue when he was thirteen, though he would became a member of the Anglican Church after his marriage. The family moved to Johannesburg when Harry

was a boy. He was educated at Charterhouse in England and Christ Church, Oxford, and served with distinction in the South African Army during the Second World War.

Harry was part of his father's empire even as a teenager and, after the war, held top positions at both Anglo American and De Beers. He took control of both companies after Sir Ernest's death in 1957. At his prime, Harry Oppenheimer was the most powerful industrialist in Africa. He died in 2000.

But our story starts in 1955, when Sir Ernest was still alive and his home was Brenthurst, the eight-hectare Oppenheimer estate in Parktown, Johannesburg. Harry and the woman he married in 1945, Bridget Denison McCall, lived at Little Brenthurst, a separate house on the same property.

At seven o'clock on the evening of 5 December 1955, Bridget Oppenheimer opened the safe in a cupboard in her bedroom and took out four pieces of jewellery to wear at dinner that night. Instead of using the key she always kept in her handbag, she used a duplicate that was kept in an old satin box in the cupboard.

She was back home by ten – husband Harry was on safari in the Congo, so she was on her own. She didn't notice anything odd, apart from a missing pillowcase. She made a mental note to speak to her personal maid, Hedwig Holman, about this, but thought no more about it. She placed the jewellery she had worn that night on the bedside table and went to sleep.

At about eight o'clock the next morning she opened the cupboard to put the four pieces of jewellery back in the safe. She was immediately alarmed when she couldn't find the satin box in which the spare key was kept. She took the other key from her handbag and opened the safe.

She went cold. The safe was empty, apart from a few inexpensive trinkets.

Gone was the unique pure white, emerald-cut, twenty-three carat diamond ring. Gone were the equally unique giant pink diamond

ring with emerald and sapphire shoulders, the rare blue marquise diamond ring, the twelve carat blue-white diamond ring set in gold and platinum. Gone, too, were the diamond and emerald necklaces, the black pearl rings, the diamond and ruby brooches and bracelets. Also missing was the unusual set of two Buddhas set in platinum and diamonds.

At the time, the collection was insured for just over £250 000, though it would fetch many millions of rands today. It was so exceptional that the Oppenheimers displayed most of the pieces in Kimberley during the British royal family's visit in 1947.

Mrs Oppenheimer telephoned the Hospital Hill police station and spoke to Captain Alwyn Burger, who, on hearing the name Oppenheimer, immediately contacted Colonel Ulf Boberg, commander of the Witwatersrand detective division. The two officers, with a small army of crack investigators, fingerprint experts and police photographers, were at Little Brenthurst before nine that morning.

Mrs Oppenheimer later admitted that her collection was too large for her to remember all the pieces, so she contacted her husband's office to obtain the list of jewellery that had been given to the insurers. This revealed that there were sixty-seven pieces in all. In addition to the police, the Brenthurst estate was also soon swarming with Anglo American employees.

Mrs Oppenheimer sent an urgent cable to Harry in the Congo. The dramatic news didn't seem to upset him too much. The next day he sent a telegram back: "Don't worry. Love. Harry."

Mrs Oppenheimer gave her first interview after the theft to Dennis Craig, a reporter at the *Star.* "I'm now left with about as much jewellery as the average city typist," she told him. He later remarked, "This was a slight exaggeration, for any office girl would have been able to 'do' the Continent on the proceeds of the pearl necklace she was wearing."

She said her most cherished piece – also, at about £700, among

the least valuable – was a brooch in the shape of a South African Tank Corps badge and studded with diamonds, which her husband had given her when he was a tank commander in the war.

Like officers Burger and Boberg, Bridget Oppenheimer was completely baffled. There was no sign of forced entry to the house and no fingerprints anywhere; nothing else was missing; and the four watchmen who had been patrolling the grounds the previous evening had noticed nothing and no one unusual. The dogs didn't bark, the butler, Robert Ritchie, didn't see or hear anything and neither did Mrs Oppenheimer's personal maid. In fact, the Oppenheimers' ten-year-old daughter, Mary, had been sleeping in the room next to her mother's and never woke up. Ritchie and Holman were grilled for hours by the detectives.

On 8 December, the crime reporter at the *Rand Daily Mail* speculated that an international gang specialising in diamond robberies "with highly-trained operatives at their command" had to be responsible. It couldn't have been an ordinary criminal or band of thieves, he wrote, because they wouldn't have been able to sell the jewellery. It must have been the same syndicate that stole jewels worth £20 000 from the Duchess of Windsor, the newspaper concluded.

On 9 December, the insurers offered a reward of £15 000 for information leading to the recovery of the Oppenheimer jewels. They announced that a senior London investigator, Dudley Strevens, would probe the theft on their behalf.

The day before Strevens arrived in Johannesburg, an Australian by the name of William Linsay Pearson walked from the Carlton Hotel in Johannesburg's city centre, where he was staying, to the insurance company's offices in Simmonds Street. He asked to see Clive Murray, the assessor who had announced the reward. Murray wouldn't see him, but was intrigued by the message Pearson left, and went to see him at the hotel later that day.

Pearson told Murray he could get the Oppenheimer jewels back,

but the insurers had to play a role in this process. Murray told him that Strevens would be leading the investigation and Pearson then insisted that he would speak only to Strevens.

The morning after his arrival from London, Dudley Strevens had a tense meeting with Colonel Ulf Boberg, who came close to threatening Strevens with arrest should he withhold any information from the police. Strevens was in fact already doing so, because he didn't tell Boberg that he was on his way to interview Pearson.

Pearson told Strevens straight off the bat that he had been a grifter all his adult life. He said he arrived in South Africa on 7 November and shortly afterwards struck up a conversation with a man in a bar. The man eventually told him that he knew of a "big job" that was going to "come off" in Johannesburg soon, and Pearson immediately assumed this would be a diamond or gold heist.

Not long after this, said Pearson, during a trip to Amsterdam and London, he read in a London newspaper that the Oppenheimer jewels had been stolen. He assumed that was the "big job" his friend had talked about.

On returning to Johannesburg, Pearson contacted the man he had met in the bar, who confirmed that his suspicions were correct. And that, said Pearson, was how he made contact with the thieves he was now offering to sell out to the insurance company.

Pearson said he could get the Oppenheimer jewellery back, but definitely not for a mere £15 000. He said he knew those who had stolen the jewellery were expecting £75 000 for it, but he could bring that down to £50 000.

Strevens responded that he could never pay more than 10 per cent of the value of the stolen goods as a reward, but added that they had increased their evaluation and could now offer him a reward of £20 000. Well, said Pearson, opening the door of his hotel room for Strevens to leave, then there was no deal to be made.

But when Strevens arrived back at his Simmonds Street office, he was told that Pearson had telephoned, saying he needed to speak

to Strevens again. At their second meeting, Pearson put a new proposal to Strevens: a reward of £20 000 and a retainer of £5 000 a year for four years as a "non-working" member of the insurance company's staff. Strevens agreed to put this proposal to his superiors in London.

Boberg became suspicious about Strevens's movements and possible contacts, and the next day, when he again threatened the insurance investigator with criminal charges, Strevens volunteered the information about Pearson. Boberg ordered Strevens to fetch Pearson at that instant.

The Australian conman repeated both his story and the proposed purchase of the jewellery for £50 000 to the colonel. Boberg cut him short, implying that Pearson was planning to steal the £50 000 and get away with the jewels as well. He had already established that Pearson could not have been the thief, since he was in Amsterdam at the time, but the police officer was in no mood to negotiate, and gave Pearson an ultimatum. The police would produce £50 000 in notes that would look real but would be worthless, having already been withdrawn from circulation. Pearson was to set a trap for the thieves, and when they took the money the police would pounce.

Pearson had little choice, and so he set the plan in motion. Boberg prepared the suitcases with the banknotes and Pearson told his contact that he was ready to buy the jewellery. He said he was acting on behalf of an Italian-American Mafia boss, Lucky Luciano, whose representative would provide the money, but would have to view the jewellery before the cash was handed over.

The trap was set for the evening of 14 December. Sergeant Johannes Swart delivered the suitcases stuffed with banknotes to Pearson's hotel room, then hid in the adjoining bathroom, pretending to be Luciano's agent. Detectives were stationed all over the hotel and police cars fitted with radios were in position throughout the neighbourhood, just in case Pearson was taking the police for a ride.

The telephone in Pearson's room rang at six minutes past nine.

Pearson stuck his head into the bathroom and told Swart the man with the jewellery would be up in fifteen minutes.

At 9.35, Pearson entered the bathroom and handed Swart a cardboard box covered in Christmas wrapping paper and tied with a chiffon scarf. In the box was the Oppenheimer collection. Sergeant Swart then put on an Italian-American accent (Sergeant Johannes Swart, imitating an Italian-American gangster, and that in 1955? I would have loved to hear that conversation!) and told Pearson loudly that he was happy and that the transaction could proceed.

Pearson went back into the bedroom, telling the men waiting there to start counting the money. Swart slipped into the corridor and signalled his colleagues, who were masquerading as hotel guests, and they stepped into Pearson's room, pistols drawn. As they entered, Pearson walked out into the corridor.

The police found two men in the room with the jewels and the money. They were both British citizens. Percival William Radley was forty-two years old and worked as the credit manager of Tropic Airways, a charter company operating between Johannesburg and Amsterdam. Donald Ernest Miles, aged thirty-four, was a former security officer with African Consolidated Theatres but currently unemployed. They were both arrested and taken to police headquarters at Marshall Square.

Boberg took the cardboard box containing the jewellery to the insurance company's offices, where they were met by Harry and Bridget Oppenheimer. Six items worth about £8 000 were missing; but the rest was all there, and real.

At the police station, Pearson had an unexpected change of heart. He professed deep remorse about selling out his friends and shouted at Boberg that he didn't want the reward and wished, instead, to be locked up with Miles and Radley. Boberg obliged. When he was searched before being placed in a cell, the police found the business card of an Amsterdam diamond-cutting factory in one of his pockets.

The three suspects were refused bail after strong representation by crack state prosecutor Dr Percy Yutar and spent Christmas in the Johannesburg prison known as The Fort, where South Africa's Constitutional Court now stands.

Pearson changed his mind again early in January, offering to be a state witness. Boberg and Yutar now had to decide whom to charge and whom to use as witnesses. They knew Pearson's story, but they interviewed the other two suspects again.

Miles offered a straightforward enough account. He said he was sitting in the lounge of the Carlton Hotel on the day of the trap when a man he knew vaguely came in and joined him for a drink. This man, whom he knew as Tony, asked him to take a parcel wrapped in Christmas paper up to room 641 as a favour. When he knocked on the door, Pearson appeared to know who "Tony" was and let him in. Radley was already in the room, said Miles.

Radley told his interrogators that Pearson had known from the start that the Oppenheimer jewels were going to be stolen. Pearson's role was to sell the stolen goods, which was why he went to England and the Netherlands shortly before the theft.

Radley proclaimed his innocence and said he was in Pearson's room when the police arrived only because Pearson had invited him for a drink. Radley now offered to turn state evidence.

Yutar and Boberg then made a decision that many legal minds argued for many years afterwards was the main reason no one was ever found guilty of stealing the Oppenheimer jewels: they decided to use Radley as a state witness and to charge Miles and Pearson with the crime. The case against Radley was formally withdrawn by Yutar on 13 January 1956.

Yutar and Boberg then sent Captain Alwyn Burger and advocate Paul Claassen, deputy attorney-general, to Europe to investigate Pearson's trip at the time of the theft. They returned empty-handed.

A man whom Radley had recommended to Pearson said he had indeed met the Australian, but they hadn't done any business

together. In Amsterdam, the investigators found that Pearson had visited diamond-cutting factories, but in every case seemed to be more interested in buying rather than selling diamonds. And in Rome, the former Mafia boss Lucky Luciano said he had never heard of Pearson in his life.

The preparatory examination, a legal procedure in use at the time to establish whether the state had a strong enough case to warrant a trial, started on 20 January 1956 before magistrate HO Cullingworth. Not even Johannesburg's largest courtroom could accommodate the number of housewives, workers, office employees and members of the business community who wanted to sneak a peek at the three suspects – and at Percy Yutar, who had been hailed as a legal genius by some court reporters.

Urban legend had it that Yutar's father had decided he should become a surgeon, but that young Percy was so determined to become a lawyer that he chopped off the fingers of his right hand in his parents' butchery. Another story was that he became a fanatical prosecuting machine after his sister was murdered. The Oppenheimer theft case dented his reputation somewhat, but it was more than fully restored (among whites, at least) when he later successfully prosecuted the Rivonia trialists: Nelson Mandela, Walter Sisulu, Govan Mbeki, Raymond Mhlaba, Andrew Mlangeni, Ahmed Kathrada, Denis Goldberg and Elias Motsoaledi. The ninth accused, Lionel Bernstein, was acquitted.

In his autobiography *Long Walk to Freedom*, Mandela said of Yutar: "He was a small, bald, dapper fellow, whose voice squeaked when he became angry or emotional. He had a flair for the dramatic and for high-flown if imprecise language."

Interestingly, when the Oppenheimer jewel case eventually went to trial, the presiding judge was Quartus de Wet – the very man who sent Mandela and his comrades to Robben Island. Of him, Mandela wrote: "He was a poker-faced judge who did not suffer fools gladly."

In 1956, Yutar told the magistrate the state would prove that while employed by a firm that insulated roofs against fire, Miles was sent to work on the roof at Little Brenthurst. He found the safe in the cupboard and the key in the box next to it, and so discovered Bridget Oppenheimer's jewellery collection.

He told his friend Radley about the jewels in April 1955. According to the prosecution, Radley had a long criminal record and thus lots of experience. In September, Radley and Miles walked through the gates of Brenthurst estate, where they were saluted by the guard, to reconnoitre the property.

They went to Little Brenthurst again a week later, the court was told, but this time entered the house – Radley demonstrated his special lock-picking talents in court – and went into the room where the jewellery was kept. But when they saw a light go on in one of the other rooms, they left. Radley then withdrew from the plan, because he thought it was too dangerous.

The state further alleged that Radley and Pearson met in the bar of the Victoria Hotel in November 1955. Radley told Pearson about the pending "big job" and asked Pearson to make contact with criminal masterminds in Europe.

The essence of the state's case was that Miles again went to Little Brenthurst on the evening of 5 December, entered the house just after Bridget Oppenheimer had left, and stole the jewellery, using the key in the satin box. Radley only learnt about the theft when he read the report in the *Star* the next day. On 7 December, Miles went to Radley's flat and told him that he had done the job, asking Radley to sell the jewels for him.

Pearson came back from Europe on 8 December and reconnected with Radley, the state alleged. Pearson then double-crossed Miles and Radley and set up the ambush in his hotel, when they were arrested by Ulf Boberg's men.

Dennis Harrison, a former colleague of Miles, testified that the latter had told him the Oppenheimer jewels were easily accessible and suggested they should go and steal them. "Miles told me that he had opened the safe with a key and seen jewellery inside," Harrison told the court. "He said the Oppenheimers were tempting a thief."

Harrison also testified that he was the one who had introduced Miles to Radley, who lived in the same block of flats and had told him that he was a long-time criminal.

Percival Radley confirmed everything Yutar presented to the court, including the fact that he met Miles through Harrison. Radley's alibi was that he was at the cinema at the time of the theft, and he had a witness who saw him there.

Radley confirmed that Miles had told him how he stole the jewellery. Miles told him he went to Little Brenthurst by bus and left the same way. That Johannesburg city bus must qualify as the most unusual getaway vehicle of all time.

The state (or the Crown, as it was known in the days before South Africa became a republic) had one more witness: Clarence Burton, a criminal who had met Pearson when both men were patients in a prison hospital. Burton said Pearson had told him how he met Radley, who talked about the imminent "big diamond job" and that he had gone to Europe to talk to potential buyers.

Burton said Pearson told him he planned to hijack the jewels from the thieves and return them to the insurance company in exchange for a reward.

The magistrate decided that there was indeed a prima facie case against the two accused and referred the matter for trial. Miles was granted bail of £5 000 but could not afford it and stayed in jail. Pearson's bail was set at £7 000, and he immediately made an urgent application to the Supreme Court for an order against the London and Lancashire Insurance Company, directing it to pay him the £20 000 reward.

The judge granted him his order and Pearson was suddenly a rich man again. He didn't get the full amount, though, as the insurers had lowered the reward to £19 202 because not all the jewellery was

recovered, and the Receiver of Revenue claimed £8 243 in income tax from Pearson.

Five weeks after the preliminary examination, the attorney-general of Transvaal decided not to prosecute Pearson for his part in the theft. The state's lawyers had concluded that they simply didn't have enough evidence against him.

If Pearson was notorious before, he now became a fully fledged Johannesburg celebrity. He was photographed wherever he went and more often than not had a reporter in tow. When he criticised Johannesburg as a "deadly dull" and ugly city, the *Rand Daily Mail* went so far as to respond in an editorial. Under the headline "A Mister Pearson", it read:

> A Mr William Linsay Pearson, who is said to come from Australia, is at present visiting Johannesburg. Mr Pearson's claim to fame is that he has received a reward of £20 000 for information he was able to give insurance assessors. Since insurance companies are not charitable institutions, those of us who are policy holders have the satisfaction of knowing that we have probably contributed to his prosperity.
>
> If Mr Pearson has any other claim to fame it seems to lie in the fact that the Attorney-General has decided not to prosecute him in a forthcoming criminal trial. This public proof of his probity, added to the reward he has earned, ought to have made his visit to Johannesburg not unsatisfactory.
>
> However, Mr Pearson is far from pleased. "I've had Johannesburg," he announced on Friday. "There's such a complete lack of anything to do that I don't think I've ever been so bored in my life ..."
>
> Some people may feel it ought to be pointed out to Mr Pearson that he has not seen Johannesburg at its best owing to the time he spent in a cell in The Fort. Others may think that he talks too much. All we have to say on the subject is that we are not interested in his views on Johannesburg, on our weather, or our race courses.

> Once certain formalities have been completed, we hope he will leave on the first available aircraft for the first country that wants him.
>
> Goodbye, Mr Pearson. You will find your hat at the bottom of the steps.

By this time, only one accused remained: Donald Ernest Miles. Of the three, he had led the most respectable life. He served in the Royal Navy, was a parachutist in the British Army and fought with the French Resistance during the Second World War. He was awarded the Distinguished Service Medal by King George VI and the Croix de Guerre by the French.

In 1947, he was working as a policeman in Palestine when he saved a young Jewish woman from being molested by a mob. Her name was Lucy and she later became his wife.

His trial, *Regina* v. *Miles*, started on 3 April 1956. Miles had chosen trial by jury, an option open to the accused in those days. After South Africa became a republic five years later, the system was abandoned in favour of verdicts by judges, sometimes serving with suitably qualified assessors such as retired magistrates.

The trial was a media frenzy, with almost all British newspapers sending their own correspondents. Members of the public queued for hours to make sure they could get seats in the courtroom.

When called to testify, Miles changed his story completely from what he had initially told Boberg. He said that when he met Radley in April 1955, he had told him about his military past and that he was out of a job. Radley said he could help Miles find a job, mentioning he was compiling a dossier for Sir Percy Sillitoe, former British intelligence chief and, at that stage, Sir Ernest Oppenheimer's security adviser.

When Radley spoke about Oppenheimer, said Miles, he claimed to have once worked at the Oppenheimer estate, specifically remarking on the lax security at Little Brenthurst. They had never spoken about this again and Miles never went to Little Brenthurst with Radley, he assured the court.

On 14 December 1955, the day of his arrest, Miles went to see Radley to find out if there was any possibility of getting a job. Radley said he would see him at his flat that evening.

When Radley arrived, Miles said, he was carrying a cardboard box wrapped in Christmas paper. He said it contained uncut diamonds. He was supposed to sell the stones on behalf of a licensed syndicate, but because the buyer was not licensed, a certain measure of risk was involved.

Miles said Radley told him to go to the Carlton Hotel with the box and telephone a Mr Pearson in room 641 at nine o'clock. Radley would answer and if he told Miles to come up for a drink, it would mean everything was fine. Radley promised him £250 for the job – money he badly needed.

Miles said he did as he was told and when he went to room 641, Pearson opened the door. He handed the gift-wrapped box to Pearson, who then carried it into the bathroom. When he came out with the box, Pearson said they should pack up. It was only then, said Miles, that he noticed the suitcases that were found to contain cash. As he bent down to pick them up, Colonel Boberg stepped into the room and arrested them.

Fred Zwarenstein, the advocate acting for Miles, asked his client who he thought stole the Oppenheimer jewels. Miles replied: "Radley obviously stole the jewels."

Miles survived rigorous cross-examination by Yutar, and then Zwarenstein began taking the prosecution's case apart, especially the testimony of Radley and Harrison. According to legal gossip at the time, Zwarenstein was brilliant at casting doubt on the evidence and painting his client as an honest and upstanding war hero.

The jury of nine white men needed only fifty-five minutes to make up their minds. In the public gallery and outside the court building, professional gamblers took bets on the outcome. By the time the jury returned, Miles was given only a five to one chance of walking out a free man.

Judge De Wet, impressive in his robes and wig, took his seat on the bench. In a loud voice in a very quiet courtroom, the registrar asked: "Gentleman of the jury, are you agreed on your verdict?"

"We are, milord," responded the foreman.

"What is your verdict?"

"Not guilty."

And the public gallery broke out in loud cheering, whistling and stamping of feet.

As Miles emerged from the court, some of the bookmakers (obviously those who made good money out of the verdict) pressed coins and banknotes into his pockets. He was met by Vera Davies, a hotel receptionist who had fallen in love with him.

The case was over, but the storm about what had gone wrong had just begun. The newspapers had a field day. The *Rand Daily Mail*'s editorial was headlined "Does crime pay?"

The *Cape Times* wrote: "As determined by the activities of the police and the law of the land, we now know of three men who did not steal the jewels, but this does not help us to know who did. The public can perhaps console itself with the thought that never in the history of spectacular crime has there been an ending so happy for so many. The crime-loving public is happy."

The *Star*, "speaking for that forgotten man, the taxpayer, who will have to bear the major cost of the prosecution", commented: "We point the finger at no particular person, nor do we question the Crown's handling of the case at any stage. But we do not imagine that the outcome can be viewed with satisfaction by anyone except, naturally, the trio most directly involved and most undeservedly glamorised, we may add, by a sensation-loving public."

The matter was even debated in parliament. Blaar Coetzee, MP for North Rand, pointed the finger at Percy Yutar. "How could the Crown have accepted the evidence of a man like Radley?" he asked.

Harry Lawrence, MP for Salt River and a former minister of justice, appeared to agree. "It is easy to be wise after the event

but, looking back, if all three men had been charged with theft or of being in possession of stolen goods, none would have escaped conviction," he said.

CR Swart, then minister of justice and later state president, heaped high praise on the police for recovering the jewels and arresting three men. He had a simple explanation for what went wrong: the jury system.

The missing jewellery, valued at £8 000, was never found or heard of again.

13

The Would-be Assassin in Green Tweed

THE DATE IS 9 APRIL 1960. THE PRIME MINISTER OF South Africa, Dr Hendrik Frensch Verwoerd, walks up to the presidential box in the grandstand after inspecting the cattle and shaking the hands of admiring farmers at the Rand Easter Show in Milner Park, Johannesburg.

It is a special occasion: the Union of South Africa is about to turn fifty. Foreign correspondents mingle with their local counterparts in the press benches, just in case Verwoerd says something newsworthy in his speech that will officially open the annual exhibition, the country's largest.

Nineteen days earlier, on 21 March, a demonstration at Sharpeville, south of Johannesburg, had gone horribly wrong. Organised by the Pan Africanist Congress in protest against the laws that forced all black adults to carry passbooks that restricted their movement and right to stay in certain areas, what was intended as a peaceful march turned into a bloodbath. The police opened fire and killed sixty-nine black demonstrators, including women and children, and injured another one hundred and eighty. On 30 March, the government declared a state of emergency, detaining some 11 700 individuals.

But the journalists hoping that the premier will say something worth reporting about these events are disappointed. Verwoerd serves

up only standard fare to his white audience. "We shall not be killed," he says to mild applause. "We shall fight for our existence, and we shall survive."

When he takes his seat next to his wife, Betsie, most reporters make their way to the press centre to phone their reports through to their newspapers. A good reporter is always reluctant to leave the scene of a news story, just in case something happens as soon as he turns his back. The *Time* magazine correspondent, Lee Griggs, remarks cynically to a few of his colleagues as they walk away: "If someone was going to shoot Verwoerd, he would have done it by now."

Minutes later, a white man in a green tweed jacket climbs the concrete steps of the grandstand in something of a hurry, flashes a card identifying him as a Rand Show VIP at Verwoerd's bodyguard and goes straight to where the prime minister is sitting. No one even notices him as he calmly steps onto a photographer's chair and says Verwoerd's name.

As Verwoerd turns to greet whoever is seeking his attention, the man produces a .22 automatic pistol and shoots the prime minister in the right cheek. Before anyone can stop him, he fires another round from less than a metre away, hitting Verwoerd in the right ear.

The wounded premier falls backwards, blood gushing from two holes in his face. His wife throws her arms around him, screaming, "What's happened?"

The president of the Witwatersrand Agricultural Society, Colonel GM Harrison, is first to realise what has happened. He leaps over a chair and knocks the pistol from the gunman's hand. By now, Verwoerd's personal bodyguard, Major Carl Richter, has also reached the assailant and helps wrestle him to the ground.

Less than a minute has lapsed since the first bullet was fired, but the word spreads quickly among spectators in the main grandstand that the prime minister has been shot. People surge forward to see what is happening, some probably trying to get their hands on the

shooter. Richter and another police officer whisk the gunman away, down the steps to the temporary police station situated within the showgrounds.

The arrested man shouts, "God help me!" as he is manhandled through the angry crowd. A police report issued afterwards states that the arrest "was made so quickly and the removal was done so quickly that an angry section of the crowd was prevented from assaulting the detainee".

The would-be assassin was taken to Marshall Square, police headquarters in Johannesburg, where he told his interrogators calmly that his name was David Beresford Pratt, that he was fifty-four years old and that he farmed cattle and trout on his property west of the city.

Verwoerd never lost consciousness and was rushed to the Johannesburg General Hospital. His cabinet colleagues and senior generals anxiously telephoned one another as they heard the news. Some went straight to the hospital. It wasn't long before doctors gave them the verdict: the prime minister's jaw was shattered in two places and his palate was punctured, but he would live.

Soon after this, Verwoerd was transferred to Pretoria's Volkshospitaal (People's Hospital), where he was treated by four top Afrikaans medical academics: professors HW Snyman, FS Oosthuizen, CH Derksen and FH Hofmeyr.

Two days later, the hospital issued a statement describing the prime minister's condition as "satisfactory". Further examinations had been carried out and confirmed "good expectations". Dr Verwoerd was resting comfortably and there was "no need for any immediate surgery".

The medical specialists later told the nation that Verwoerd's survival was a miracle. Had Pratt used a larger calibre weapon than a .22, one bullet would have penetrated the temple bone and lodged in the prime minister's brain. As it was, however, the surgeons removed the two bullets without any complications and Verwoerd suffered no medium- or long-term damage as a result of being shot.

His more fanatical followers firmly believed that Verwoerd's miraculous survival was confirmation that God had saved him to serve his people – a notion he did nothing to dispel. The incident enhanced the hero-worship that the majority of white Afrikaners had for him.

"With two bullet wounds to his face, his chances of recovery appeared slim," wrote Senator MPA Malan in the 1964 publication *Die Nasionale Party van Suid-Afrika: Sy Stryd en Prestasies.* "With the strength he had been given, he recovered quickly and resumed his duties as if no disaster had befallen him. He is physically strong, but it is the spiritual strength with which he has been blessed that makes him capable of great things."

Two days after the failed assassination attempt, cabinet minister and National Party stalwart Paul Sauer told the white parliament in an emotional address that South Africans should be ashamed at such behaviour from within their ranks. The leader of the official opposition, Sir De Villiers Graaff, tabled a motion of support and sympathy.

On 29 May, Verwoerd officially returned to his office. Two days later, he delivered an address at the huge mass gathering in Bloemfontein to commemorate half a century of unity.

Senator Malan wrote: "A grateful *volk* [nation] bowed its head [in gratitude] at the miracle that their Leader was saved and that he could continue to serve his people. The Father in Heaven was thanked for his recovery."

A year after the Union of South Africa's fiftieth birthday, and following the National Party's victory in a referendum, Verwoerd led the country out of the British Commonwealth and declared it a republic, enhancing his status among his followers even more.

Pratt's attempt to kill Verwoerd has often been referred to as the first attempted or actual assassination in South Africa's history. This is not correct. For example, the legendary Zulu king Shaka was assassinated on 24 September 1828 in his royal residence, KwaDukuza,

by his half-brothers Dingane and Mhlangana, assisted by Shaka's assistant, Mbopha. More than one hundred and sixty years later, on 10 April 1993, another prominent political figure, Communist Party leader Chris Hani, would be gunned down by Polish immigrant Janus Walusz.

Hani's murder plunged South Africa into a crisis that threatened the fragile negotiations designed to create a democracy and end apartheid, the system that was so assiduously cultivated by Verwoerd and other National Party leaders over almost fifty years. Swift action by the police and political intervention by Nelson Mandela helped to calm the situation: the talks resumed, Mandela became the country's first black president and Hani's killer was jailed for life, along with a right-wing politician, Clive Derby-Lewis, who was found to have supplied the murder weapon.

More than three decades earlier David Pratt, a respected member of the Witwatersrand Agricultural Society, appeared in the Johannesburg Magistrates' Court on 11 April 1960. He was sent for psychological evaluation and in September was declared mentally disturbed and not fit to stand trial. He was held at Pretoria Central Prison before being confined at the mental hospital in Bloemfontein.

Pratt was born in England and educated at Cambridge University. In a feature on his attempt to kill Verwoerd, *Time* magazine referred to him as a "gentle, kind man who collects guns", but added that he had a history of epilepsy and a tendency towards sudden violence. "Last year, after his Dutch wife left him for another man, he arrived at Amsterdam's airport with a gun in his pocket and proclaimed his intention of killing her."

Pratt hanged himself in his hospital ward with a bed sheet on 1 October 1961. At the time, his suicide was likened to that of Judas Iscariot, the man who betrayed Jesus Christ and then hanged himself from a tree. Several writers subsequently suggested that Pratt was unlikely to have killed himself, but no evidence has ever surfaced to indicate that he was, in fact, murdered.

Before his death, Pratt offered some insight into his thinking through notes that he left and during conversations with friends, family members and psychiatrists. He said that in 1954 he had heard organ music playing in his head and often felt disembodied. He sought help and was sent to an institution that specialised in nervous disorders, but he became violent and had to be locked in a padded cell.

Pratt claimed that during his incarceration he entered into a "Miltonian hell, complete with fires, prongs, and yells of anguish". He saw the universe as a piece of theatre and all human beings as actors. He developed an obsessive hatred of Afrikaner nationalism and started seeing himself as a biblical prophet called upon to sacrifice his own life.

He was treated for extreme depression, and in 1959 his state of mind altered dramatically – "the grass looked greener and the birds sang more sweetly", he said.

The day before he shot Verwoerd, Pratt saw black prisoners being bundled into a police van. It depressed him to think about what would happen to them. The next morning, he said, "the feeling became very strong that someone in the country must do something about it, and it better bloody well be me, feeling as I do about it."

Before leaving home to attend the Rand Easter Show, he put a .22 pistol in his pocket, though he had no specific plan or intention to use it. Pratt, who was seated almost immediately next to Verwoerd in the VIP section during the opening ceremony at the show, said he was angry at the audience's neutral reaction to the premier's speech. "If there had been strong booing, it would have been sufficient."

When he appeared in court, Pratt said: "I won't go through the shooting sequence, except to say that I felt a violent urge to shoot apartheid, the stinking apartheid monster gripping South Africa."

After firing the two shots, he felt a tremendous release of tension. "I had my best night's sleep in six years. From then until now I have spent my life in the isolation of a cell with short exercise breaks. Five

months seldom seeing the sun, conditions I have never experienced. Yet these few months have been a hundred times happier than the past five years."

Pratt became something of a hero among certain anti-apartheid activists, who loved to quote him saying, "If you know you must do something and you don't do it, you are not free." Shooting "the epitome of apartheid" had evidently set him free.

A week after the shooting, *Time* magazine observed: "The nation's Africans could be thankful that the assassin was white. If he had been black, a bloodbath might have followed. For the blacks, the week had already been bitter enough as Verwoerd's police and troops relentlessly worked to stamp out the dying embers of revolt. Chief quarry was the ringleaders who still urged blacks to stay at home rather than return to their jobs in white men's shops and factories."

Verwoerd, who was born in the Dutch capital of Amsterdam on 8 September 1901, is often referred to as "the architect of apartheid", but that's a bit of a misnomer. In truth, racial separation, disenfranchisement and oppression of black people dates back to the earliest European colonialists and was formalised by Britain when the Union of South Africa was formed in 1910, with virtually no civil rights for black people.

But Verwoerd did take apartheid to a new level, advancing the idea that blacks were not South Africans but should live in their own independent bantustans, and attaching a quasi-religious intellectual justification to the policy of segregation.

This made him one of the most resented human beings in South Africa, Africa and the international community. No wonder, then, that he became the target of another assassin, six years after Pratt shot him.

At 2.15 p.m. on 6 September 1966, Verwoerd was stabbed to death in his seat in parliament. His killer was a uniformed parliamentary messenger, Dimitri Tsafendas.

Verwoerd's wife was again an eyewitness – Betsie watched the

stabbing from the wives' gallery and ran down to where he was lying on the floor. She kissed him before he was taken to Groote Schuur Hospital, where he was certified dead on arrival.

Tsafendas went on trial for the murder on 17 October 1966, but only three days into proceedings Mr Justice Beyers declared the accused "insane and unfit to stand trial". He had been diagnosed as suffering from paranoid schizophrenia and had a persistent delusion that a giant tapeworm was eating him up from inside.

Tsafendas spent the rest of his life in jail, where he died in October 1999.

14

Escape from the Island (*Part 2*)

ROBBEN ISLAND WAS USED AS A PRISON FOR MOST OF the time between 1652 and 1921, although it also served as a leper colony and a lunatic asylum during this period. After 1921 it was used by the army and navy as a training centre and coastal defence position. From 1961 to 1991 it was again used as a prison, for ordinary criminals as well as political prisoners.

During this thirty-year period, escape was on the minds of many, as it had been in Makhanda's time. Two political prisoners who seem to have had more of an obsession with freedom than the others are Eddie Daniels of the Liberal Party and Mac Maharaj, a senior African National Congress and Umkhonto we Sizwe leader.

"From day one of my arrest I dreamt of escaping," writes Daniels in his book *There and Back: Robben Island 1964–1979*. He first tried to escape from Pollsmoor Prison in Cape Town after paying a warder to smuggle a few hacksaw blades into his cell, but the sawn-through bars were discovered before the men could make a run for it.

Escape from the political section of the Robben Island prison was virtually impossible, says Daniels. There were headcounts of the inmates early in the morning before they went out to work, at each of the three gates they had to pass through, again once they were outside, every thirty minutes at the work site, at the end of the day before going back and again at each of the three gates. Back in the yard outside the cells, they had to strip naked and their clothes were

searched. They would again be counted once in their cells. A warder was locked in with them and the lights were kept on all night.

Early on during his incarceration, Daniels sneaked a letter to Sedick Isaacs, a Pan Africanist Congress prisoner in another section, asking him when the best time of year would be to escape. Isaacs, a science and geography teacher, told him winter was the best, because the tides would carry a swimmer to the mainland.

The same Sedick planned to poison the water reservoir on the island, so as to force the transfer of all prisoners to the mainland, from where it would be easier to escape. The warders discovered his plan and sentenced him to an extra nine months in prison and six cuts.

Daniels says the best of all the plans he cooked up while on Robben Island involved a sturdy log and spades. He was in charge of maintaining the shed at the quarry where the political prisoners worked, and he had built a birdbath to make it look more attractive. The bath consisted of a washbasin in a sandpit, bordered by four large logs.

"The idea was that if the opportunity occurred, that is if we could get at least ten hours before we were discovered missing, we would trundle one of those logs down to the nearby beach on a wheelbarrow from the tool shed," Daniels writes. "Using spades as oars, we would paddle across to Bloubergstrand on the mainland, about 7 km away. We would tie the spades to our bodies with strips of blanket, to prevent us losing them, and also wrap strips of blanket around our legs, so we would not cut ourselves while paddling."

Daniels eventually abandoned the plan because they could never find an opportunity to see if the log would indeed work, or a chance to put the escape into action.

His next escape plan was supposed to take place in 1981, after his own release. The first version would have had a helicopter pick up certain prisoners and take them to a foreign warship just outside South African waters. But Daniels couldn't be sure that the South African government would not simply ignore international law and confront the ship anyway.

No, Daniels decided, the helicopter had to fly directly to Cape Town and land at a foreign embassy sympathetic to the ANC, where they would seek asylum. Not even the apartheid government would dare storm the grounds of a foreign embassy, he reckoned.

The plan became his consuming obsession. He was due for release in November 1979, so he would coordinate the escape from outside. His intention was to rescue the ANC's two elder statesmen on the island, Nelson Mandela and Walter Sisulu. Sisulu later informed Daniels that Mandela would go alone, because one of them had to remain on the island in a leadership role.

Mandela himself was keen on the plan, says Daniels, and told him: "We are revolutionaries. It is our duty to try and escape the clutches of the enemy."

The escape was planned for New Year's Day 1981. The public holiday was chosen deliberately, because it was a visiting day, most prisoners would be watching a film in the hall with free access to the yard, and security would generally be a bit more relaxed.

The ANC would hire a helicopter with a winch and cable attached to a basket big enough for two people. The basket would be adorned with South Africa's orange, white and blue flag and streamers to make it look festive and to discourage guards from shooting at it.

On the morning of 1 January, Daniels and the pilot would take off from Cape Town and fly to the island, timing it so they would be above the prison by 9.15. The authorities would only become concerned at the last minute, because many helicopters flew over the island regularly. If they were contacted by radio and asked about their flight plan, Daniels would have the pilot say they were well-wishers bringing presents to the warders.

Mandela would be waiting in the courtyard when the helicopter arrived and the basket was lowered. Other prisoners who knew of the plan would rush out, blocking the corridor as if curious, and so prevent the warders from getting outside. In any case, the warders didn't carry arms inside the political section.

Mandela would climb into the basket and the helicopter would fly straight to Cape Town as fast as possible. The plan relied heavily on the likelihood of great confusion on the island, which would give them a few minutes to get away. The distance was too short for the air force to scramble attack aircraft.

The helicopter would land in the grounds of a foreign embassy and Daniels and Mandela would simply run into the nearest building and ask for asylum.

It was a simple plan and one with a fair chance of success – if a pilot could be found who would cooperate. There was no doubt that one of the foreign embassies in Cape Town would have been amenable to accepting Mandela – even the United States would have done so, because Jimmy Carter was president at the time.

The plan was endorsed by the ANC's High Command on the island, on condition that the High Command in exile also accepted it. Arrangements for Daniels to meet ANC leader Oliver Tambo in Botswana after his release to coordinate the plan were thwarted when Daniels was placed under house arrest.

Daniels did, however, succeed in smuggling out the plan (on thin paper hidden between the layers of an ordinary postcard) and getting it to Tambo via London. That was the last that Daniels heard of the plan for thirteen years.

After the unbanning of the ANC and the release of Mandela and other political prisoners in 1990, Daniels at last learnt what had happened to his brainchild.

The ANC High Command in Lusaka had indeed received the plan and were discussing it when they received information of an impending South African raid on their offices. They decided to destroy the plan with all other strategic documentation to prevent it being discovered by the security forces.

A leading member of the Dutch Anti-Apartheid Movement, Connie Braam, who was present at this meeting, had the presence of mind to rescue the piece of paper outlining the plan and took it with her to Holland.

Eddie Daniels saw his plan in his own handwriting in 1993, when it was exhibited in a Cape Town museum.

In his autobiography *Long Walk to Freedom*, Mandela tells the story of the day one of the Robben Island warders left his key on the desk in the warder's office in the political section of the prison. The "master craftsman" among the political prisoners, Jeff Masemola, made an imprint of the key on a piece of soap. Using the outline, he filed a key from a piece of metal that unlocked most of the doors in the section where they were kept. "But we never used it to leave our section," Mandela writes. "It was the sea, after all, that was the uncrossable moat around Robben Island."

Mac Maharaj was the other Robben Island inmate who always had escape on his mind. He had discussed this with Mandela and Sisulu, who accepted in principle that he would be planning an escape, but said he had to take one of them with him.

Maharaj tells the story of his best escape plan in *Shades of Difference: Mac Maharaj and the Struggle for South Africa*, the biography written by Padraig O'Malley. In 1973, accompanied by two warders, Maharaj was taken to Cape Town to see a dentist. While sitting in the dentist's chair, he complained about the fact that he had to remain shackled and handcuffed when receiving medical attention. The dentist asked the guard to remove the restraints.

Then Maharaj complained that it was unacceptable to be treated by a dentist in the presence of someone who was not a dental assistant. The dentist asked the warder to leave the room.

The warder's compliance set Maharaj's mind racing: this would be the best place from which to stage an escape. Back on the island, he persuaded Mandela and others (according to Mandela the only other person was Wilton Mkwayi) to make appointments with the dentist. Maharaj knew a taxi driver based at the Parade in Cape Town, Tofi Bardien, who would be recruited to help them get away.

Five months after he hatched the plan in the dentist's chair, the three men were taken to Cape Town by boat and loaded into a prison van.

Maharaj says he searched the van and found a knife in a crevice. "I showed it to the others, and we all became excited because we had been wondering how to overwhelm the warders. I hid the knife in my pocket. We were very tense, and I had a great sense of alertness."

When they got to the dentist, the waiting room was empty. The warders took the handcuffs off the prisoners, and, while they were waiting, Maharaj stood at the window, looking down at the street.

He suddenly became very suspicious. On his previous visit, the street below had been a hive of activity, with many cars and people coming and going. Now not a soul could be seen. Maharaj beckoned Mandela to the window and showed him the quiet street. It was a trap, he said. Mandela agreed and said they should abandon the escape plan.

After their treatment they were put back into the van, but were taken to Roeland Street Jail instead of back to the island. Maharaj suspected that the cell in which they were placed was bugged and scribbled a note to the others not to talk about their plans. After a while they were taken back to the island.

Back in their section they agreed that the prison authorities must have bugged their cells, heard of their escape plan and then planted the knife in the van. Maharaj believed the authorities wanted them to escape, so that they could shoot and kill Mandela.

Was this pure paranoia, or is it possible that the security bosses of the time could actually have planned to kill the most famous prisoner in their custody?

Well, yes. That was exactly what the oddball chief of the Bureau of State Security (BOSS), General Lang Hendrik van den Bergh, had planned just three years before Maharaj devised his little escapade at the dentist's rooms. The bizarre story was first revealed by the former BOSS agent who doubled as a journalist, Gordon Winter, in his 1981 book *Inside BOSS: South Africa's Secret Police*, and more recently retold by James Sanders in *Apartheid's Friends: The Rise and Fall of South Africa's Secret Service*.

Robert Bruce was an old friend and former client of Nelson Mandela's in Johannesburg. On 18 March 1969, Bruce had this notice published in *The Times* of London: "I seek a person determined to pursue world embracing loyalties beyond national commitments; based London; adventurous; good contact and liaison; personality, competent organiser, prepared to execute unusual work in spare time without financial reward."

One of Van den Bergh's British sources told him that the message could have some South African connection, and the boss of BOSS instructed Winter to investigate.

Winter responded to the notice and so discovered Bruce's rather naïve ambition to rescue Mandela from Robben Island. He wanted Mandela to eventually rule South Africa as leader of a "new multi-racial party of national liberation" and then have the headquarters of the United Nations transferred to South Africa to "enhance the UN's moral power".

Bruce believed that Mandela's only chance of escape was by air, and he asked Winter to find a pilot. Winter played along and recruited renowned British aviatrix Sheila Scott, who actually flew her plane all the way to Cape Town.

Van den Bergh's plan to kill Mandela without incurring the wrath of the international community went like this. A Robben Island prison warder, Gideon Huisamen, would drug his fellow warders and get Mandela out of the cells. A rescue party with a high-speed motorboat would pick him up on the nearby beach and race him to the mainland. From there he would be taken to a remote landing strip, where the aircraft would be waiting.

Mandela would be given a revolver, but it would be loaded only with blanks, so he wouldn't be able to shoot anyone. As he approached the plane, he would be shot dead by policemen. Real bullets would then be put in his revolver.

Van den Bergh believed this was a foolproof way to get rid of Mandela and blame his death on the recklessness of British radicals.

But in August 1970, Bruce inadvertently told someone linked to MI6, Britain's agency for espionage, counter-espionage and covert action overseas, of the plan and they figured out who was behind it. Van den Bergh was immediately warned to back off and he then ordered Winter to abandon the plan.

Imagine South Africa without Nelson Mandela for the past twenty years …

15

The Head of the Snake

THE TIME: JUST AFTER 8 A.M. ON MONDAY 15 OCTOBER 1992.

The place: the offices of *Vrye Weekblad* in Bree Street, Newtown, Johannesburg.

A young reporter, Pearlie Joubert, arrives at work. Waiting at the office entrance to see someone from the newspaper are two men. One is the owner of a restaurant in Rockey Street, Yeoville; the other is a Mozambican citizen and former worker at the restaurant.

His name is João Alberto Cuna, although he also has a South African identity document in the name of Malefetsane Johanne Mokoena.

The confusing story he told *Vrye Weekblad* that Monday morning would cause high drama and lead to a severe crisis in FW de Klerk's National Party government two months later – a crisis that some would say came close to a military coup, because twenty-three top South African Defence Force (SADF) officers were fired as a result.

I was a supporting actor in this drama, as at the time, I was the editor of *Vrye Weekblad*, an independent Afrikaans-language newspaper with a strong reputation for exposing the realities of the apartheid system and the excesses of its security forces.

During the late 1980s and early 1990s, we spent considerable time and energy trying to establish who and what the "Third Force" was – the sinister, secretive force that continued to foment conflict between especially the main ethnic party in KwaZulu-Natal, the

Inkatha Freedom Party, and the ANC and its internal sister movement, the United Democratic Front (UDF). More than 15 000 people died in this conflict between 1985 and 1994.

In the same edition of *Vrye Weekblad* that carried Cuna's first story, we published a report of the massacre of eleven people at Umgababa in KwaZulu-Natal, perpetrated by unknown killers. This was the face of the conflict: random attacks on groups of people in their homes and the killing of passengers on suburban trains by unidentified assailants.

The old defence force, the South African Police (SAP) and the government itself vehemently denied that there was any such thing as a Third Force or that any one of them had an agenda to destabilise the political atmosphere on the eve of negotiations for a democratic settlement, or to poison interaction between black parties.

But this changed the moment João Cuna opened his mouth.

This is the remarkable story of how a scared young man from Mozambique unknowingly blew the cover off a highly secretive and nasty unit of the apartheid government's security forces.

Cuna, who was twenty-nine years old in 1992, said he had deserted from the Mozambique army in 1987 and fled to South Africa to seek work. Not long after his arrival in Johannesburg, another Mozambican took him to a café in Maddison Street, Jeppe, where he met the Schultz family, who had a room that Cuna could rent. He lived there for a few years.

Late in 1991, one of the Schultz men, named Boy, saw a FRELIMO army badge that Cuna had kept, and asked him about his past. When Cuna told him he was a former soldier, Schultz said he had a job for his lodger.

At the end of October or the beginning of November 1991, Schultz took him to a building in Pretoria. Cuna couldn't tell *Vrye Weekblad* the address, as he didn't know Pretoria at all, but he said it was a tall building with men in uniform at the entrance.

In his limited English, Cuna explained that he was introduced

to a "big, fat white man" who asked him whether he liked the ANC or the Inkatha Freedom Party. Cuna responded that he didn't know anything about either. The man promised him lots of money if he joined the ANC in Yeoville and spied on them from within. He said Cuna should also visit known ANC houses in other suburbs and report on people's movements and whether they had any firearms. Cuna said he would do it.

According to Cuna, Schultz then took him to the Johannesburg Sun Hotel. "There were six white men in the room. The one introduced himself as a farmer from Natal. The others didn't speak. I can't remember any of their names, but I would recognise them if I saw them again," Cuna told *Vrye Weekblad.*

"The farmer said he was going to take me to Natal and that I had to go and kill ANC members. He asked if I could plant a bomb. I said I would do the work for him."

But Cuna didn't really want to do this "work". He agreed only because he was scared of the men at the hotel. The very next day, he ran away and went to stay with a friend in Bertrams.

But Schultz tracked him down and took him to the Casablanca Roadhouse in Hillbrow, where Schultz and the "farmer" gave him R2 000 to spend on anything he wanted. "I told them I did not like the work, but I would do it because I was afraid of them," said Cuna.

Around the end of March 1992, Schultz and the "farmer" fetched Cuna in a white Nissan. They travelled to Pietermaritzburg and stayed in a smart hotel, where there were "lots of rich white people". They were joined by another white man who was supposed to look after Cuna, and the men gave Cuna new clothes and presents.

A few days later, Schultz and the "farmer" took him to Durban. In the car was another black man who spoke Portuguese, but also some Zulu. Cuna couldn't remember his name.

At about 7.30 that evening, the four of them went to a large, face-brick building. It could have been a police station, said Cuna, because there were men in uniform at the gate. But then he added that all

the people he saw outside the building were soldiers in brown uniforms.

A white man came out of the building and they all got into a cream-coloured minibus with tinted windows. They followed the directions of the other black man. Cuna didn't know the name of the township, but he could describe the area and the house they went to. The "farmer" said the people in the house were all ANC members. Cuna continued his story:

> The other black man and I first scouted the area while the men sat waiting in the kombi at a taxi rank. When we got back into the kombi, we were each given a balaclava, an AK47 rifle and ammunition which they had stored under the back seat.
>
> Me, the other black man and the white man who was picked up at the brick building then put balaclavas over our faces. The white men also had dark glasses and balaclavas on.
>
> We drove past the house four times and then the farmer dropped us off. We got out and ran up to the windows. The white man went to a back window. I saw between seven and nine people inside the house. They were standing there talking. Most of the people were men but there were a few women as well.
>
> We then started firing. I saw people falling and they were screaming. One man ran away. I only saw him when he was already far away. I do not know how he got outside the house.
>
> We then stopped firing. I do not know whether everybody inside the house was dead. We did not go inside. We stopped firing and ran back to the kombi that the farmer was driving around.
>
> We got inside the kombi and went back to the taxi rank. There the three of us, except for the driver, shot through the back windows at people who were still at the rank. I shot three people but I am not certain about this because the farmer was driving very fast.

They then drove back to the face-brick building to drop off the white man who had joined them earlier, left their balaclavas and rifles there and returned to Pietermaritzburg. Schultz, the "farmer" and Cuna went back to Johannesburg the next day, where he was given R4 000.

"I didn't want to kill anybody," Cuna told us. "I was forced to kill. I don't hate the ANC, I don't hate Inkatha. I don't even know who they are. The white people dragged me into this. I was afraid of them and then I said yes. I don't want to kill anyone. This thing has made me tired of life. I don't care what happens, I just want to get out of this mess."

Schultz organised a passport for Cuna in the name of Malefetsane Johanne Mokoena. According to the document, issued on 22 April 1992, Cuna was born in South Africa on 2 June 1964. He used the passport to go to Mozambique, where he gave most of the money he received for the killings to his mother.

That was Cuna's story. My colleagues and I had to ask ourselves whether he was telling the truth; was he perhaps a nutcase or even a plant by the security forces in an effort to trap and embarrass us?

His employer said Cuna told him the same story he told us but never asked to be taken to a newspaper. He simply asked his boss to help him, because the men who took him to Durban wanted him to go on another killing spree, and he didn't want to kill any more people. It was his employer's idea to approach *Vrye Weekblad.* He thought making Cuna's story public would ensure his safety, and he knew that ours was the only newspaper with the guts to do this kind of story, he said.

The problem was that Cuna couldn't give us exact dates and places that we could check. We did ask a church organisation with good knowledge of local events and people to help, and they pointed to five attacks, very similar to the one Cuna described, between the end of March and mid-April 1992 in the KwaGcaba and Murchison areas outside Durban.

Pearlie Joubert then found out that Schultz was indeed a policeman, something he at first denied. His name was Joseph, although people also called him Boy or Harold. His mother eventually admitted to Pearlie that he was stationed at John Vorster Square, police headquarters in Johannesburg, and later that day Pearlie saw Schultz being dropped off by colleagues in a car with a police registration plate.

Our theory at the time was that the white men who took Cuna to Pietermaritzburg must have been security policemen. Then my colleague Jacques Pauw had an idea: show Cuna photographs of policemen whom we knew were involved in dirty tricks or hit squad activities. Jacques spread the photographs out on the office floor, and when Cuna saw the face of Ferdi Barnard he said: "That's the man who took me to Durban."

Now another possibility presented itself: could the "farmer" and the other white men have been members of the SADF's nefarious and covert Civil Cooperation Bureau (or CCB) to which we knew Barnard had connections?

It so happened that the judicial inquest into the assassination on 1 May 1989 of anti-apartheid activist and academic David Webster was taking place in the Johannesburg Supreme Court at this time. Barnard was the prime suspect, but in fact he was only convicted of the murder some years later. Perhaps I should digress and tell a little bit about that.

On 23 October 1996, Jacques and I, both working for the SABC after *Vrye Weekblad* shut down in February 1994, had lunch with Barnard at a fancy fish restaurant in Seventh Street, Melville. Jacques had been building contact with Barnard over a long period and I was going along as a witness and a form of insurance.

Barnard was visibly high on some drug, probably cocaine, because his head was bobbing up and down and he was talking far too much.

At some point, Jacques and Barnard left the restaurant and went to Barnard's car, parked in the street. While smoking a crack pipe, Barnard confessed to Jacques that he did, in fact, kill Webster.

He had shot him in front of his house and watched his body "fly through the air and land on the pavement". He was paid a R40 000 "production bonus" by the CCB, he said, and the CCB commander, Joe Verster, knew about the whole operation.

Soon afterwards, Jacques made an affidavit about Barnard's confession, and in September 1997 the killer was arrested, tried and found guilty as charged. It was his fourth murder conviction. As I write, he is still in jail.

But when Cuna identified Barnard's photograph in October 1992, we knew only that he was a suspect in the Webster murder and that he had something to do with the assassination of my old friend Anton Lubowksi in Namibia. We also knew that Barnard had worked with the notorious Brixton Murder and Robbery Squad, that he had spent time in jail for murder and that he had CCB connections.

When Cuna picked out Barnard, we knew he was authentic. We published his confession and photograph as a cover story on 30 October 1992 under the headline "At last proof of the Third Force".

In my weekly editorial comment, I pleaded with then state president FW de Klerk to face the fact that Cuna's story was proof that a Third Force was indeed undermining peace and stability during the negotiations period. Too many people were dying in KwaZulu-Natal, and it was in De Klerk's power to put an end to the killing.

We knew that if the police or whoever else made Cuna take part in these shootings found out that he was talking to us, his life would be worthless, so while we were grilling Cuna and verifying his story, he stayed with Pearlie at a house in Bertrams, not far from the home of Boy Schultz.

De Klerk had already appointed Judge Richard Goldstone to lead a commission of inquiry into state-sponsored political violence and death squads, so we contacted Major Frank Dutton, one of the policemen working with Goldstone and whom we trusted, to take care of Cuna and investigate his story.

But on the Monday after publication, Cuna disappeared without

trace. When he reappeared two days later, he told Pearlie that he had a great new story for us.

He described a house in Muller Street, Yeoville, where he had met with his white "handlers" and an Indian man. They planned further random attacks on people in KwaZulu-Natal at these meetings, Cuna said, describing the house and the layout of the rooms in great detail.

This would indeed have given us a brand-new angle on the story, so Pearlie went to the house Cuna described. She rang the bell at the gate for hours, but nobody reacted. However, she could hear the sounds of people in the house, so she tried another tactic. She rang the bell and started screaming for help at the same time.

An Indian man did indeed appear at the gate, and Pearlie couldn't believe her eyes. She immediately recognised him as Mac Maharaj, senior ANC and Umkhonto we Sizwe leader, who would serve as a minister in Nelson Mandela's first cabinet in 1994. Mac invited Pearlie in and she told him the whole story. She immediately realised that Cuna's description of the interior of the house was completely correct.

Mac tells the story in Padraig O'Malley's book *Shades of Difference: Mac Maharaj and the Struggle for South Africa.* Armed with Pearlie's information, he confronted the Goldstone Commission, because he knew Cuna was going to retell all his stories to Goldstone's investigators.

> The Goldstone investigators came to see me. They indicated that they didn't believe Cunas's [Mac incorrectly calls him Cunas] story but were obliged to question me. He had described a room in my house where these meetings had allegedly taken place. We agreed that certain questions should be put to this man in my presence.
>
> Then they pulled a trick on me. I went to Pretoria to meet the Goldstone Commission people in their offices. Unbeknownst to me, they had this Cunas in the foyer of their building so I would see him as I arrived. They wanted to see if I would recognise him. As I walked in, they were watching me.

> But I'd never seen the man before; I didn't even look at him. They could see from my lack of reaction that I didn't recognise Cunas. My evidence of denial was accepted by the commission and Cunas's allegations came to nothing.

As far as I could determine, it was never officially established who had gotten to Cuna during his brief disappearance and made him tell these lies. My theory is that the same people who took him on the killing spree to Durban realised that after he had been linked to the Third Force in *Vrye Weekblad*, he could be a good man to plant some disinformation.

We know that the SADF, the SAP and indeed the last apartheid establishment hated Maharaj with a passion and wanted to either kill or discredit him. About a year after this incident, the police "leaked" a story to some newspapers linking Maharaj to a car hijacking syndicate. The police and the newspapers had to apologise afterwards.

Whoever they were, these people didn't bargain on *Vrye Weekblad*'s meticulousness when it came to major revelations – we were always conscious of the possibility of the security forces themselves planting a story on us. We had earlier blown the cover off the police death squads working out of Vlakplaas, a farm outside Pretoria, exposed the CCB and published numerous other revelations of dirty tricks and assassinations, so we knew they would have loved to nail us somehow.

Pearlie Joubert and Frank Dutton then took Cuna on a drive through the streets of Pretoria, in the hope that he might recognise the buildings he had been taken to by his "handlers", one of whom he had by now identified as Ferdi Barnard. They were not surprised when he pointed out Wachthuis, police headquarters, but they thought he was mistaken when he showed them a building called Momentum Mews in the suburb of Faerie Glen. It appeared to be nothing more than an ordinary office block. It turned out to be something else entirely.

Judge Goldstone asked Dutton and another policeman, Colonel

Henk Heslinga, to investigate Cuna's claims and allegations. Heslinga took Cuna to Pietermaritzburg and from one hotel to another, until Cuna recognised the fancy establishment where they had stayed before the massacre he had told us about. It was the Hilton Hotel, and Cuna now also remembered that the man he had identified as Ferdi Barnard used the name Frank Smith on their trip.

Following what turned out to be a good hunch, Heslinga asked the hotel manager to show him all the credit card slips for the period Cuna was talking about. Among them, he found a Diners Club slip in the name of Frank Smith of Africa Risk Analysis Consultants (ARAC).

Heslinga approached Diners Club for more information about ARAC and Smith, but was told they could not divulge any details about their customers. This was where Judge Richard Goldstone came in. "I decided that this was an appropriate case in which to implement the powers of search and seizure given to me by the commission's statute," he writes in *For Humanity: Reflections of a War Crimes Investigator.*

> The firm of attorneys where I had served articles of clerkship many years before acted for Diners Club. I contacted a partner, who handled the account, and informed him that I needed the information in question but that I preferred to obtain the information informally rather than send in investigators who would have to seize the records.
>
> Within minutes I received a call from the managing director of Diners Club, who informed me that a warrant should be faxed to him. Thereafter he would immediately give our investigators the information required.
>
> He added that ARAC was their largest customer and that he hoped we would not close them down. Over forty cards were listed in the names of ARAC employees, and millions of rands were spent annually on transport and hotel expenses. I knew at that moment that we were onto something big.

The registered business address of Africa Risk Analysis Consultants was Momentum Mews, Faerie Glen, Pretoria.

Goldstone decided to appoint advocate Torie Pretorius of the attorney-general's office to lead the raid on ARAC's premises – he was "a very competent lawyer and an excellent investigator," says Goldstone. Pretorius was accompanied by Heslinga and fifteen uniformed policemen, requested by Goldstone, as well as a number of European police officers who were in South Africa as international observers during the negotiation process. The raid was to take place on 11 November 1992.

What Goldstone didn't know – and what I learnt only in 2007 when a journalist by the name of De Wet Potgieter published a book called *Total Onslaught: Apartheid's Dirty Tricks Exposed* – was that Heslinga was playing a double role. "He had been ordered by the police generals to act as informant on the Goldstone Commission's activities," writes Potgieter, adding that Heslinga confirmed this in a subsequent interview. Judging by Goldstone's glowing praise for Heslinga, he had no idea when he wrote his own book in 2000 that Heslinga was a mole.

According to Potgieter, when Goldstone asked Pretorius and Heslinga to raid ARAC's offices, Heslinga immediately informed the head of the SAP's detectives, General Johan le Roux. Le Roux in turn notified General Witkop Badenhorst, head of Military Intelligence, who was reportedly not alarmed "and commented that it was probably a bunch of rebel ex-Rhodesians who were involved in some or other shit".

On arrival at ARAC's offices, Pretorius and Heslinga produced the search warrant issued by Goldstone. It soon became clear to them that ARAC was a front for a division of Military Intelligence called the Directorate Covert Collection (DCC).

The truth was out. Ferdi Barnard was an agent for a Military Intelligence front company and was responsible for massacres and other activities that had long been ascribed to a Third Force.

Pretorius phoned Goldstone with the news, and the judge ordered him to demand the unit's files on Barnard.

"I realised that if I had ordered a general search, it would have led to an urgent court proceeding and that we would have had little prospect of justifying a fishing expedition," says Goldstone. He did immediately inform the minister of justice, Kobie Coetsee, who told him: "Judge, you must do what you have to do."

It wasn't long before General Badenhorst himself and the chief director of DCC, Brigadier Tolletjie Botha, arrived on the scene. According to Potgieter, Heslinga told Botha that the raid was a result of the reports in *Vrye Weekblad*, to which Botha replied, "I don't read that fucking newspaper."

Botha had no choice but to allow the Goldstone team access to his vaults, from which they removed five files relating only to Ferdi Barnard. These included documents mentioning João Cuna, as well as indications that Cuna might have been involved with Barnard in gun-running from Mozambique.

One document revealed Operation Baboon, a plan to gather information that could be used to blackmail senior ANC leaders and anti-apartheid activists. This information solved the mystery of who had spirited Cuna away from Pearlie Joubert's house and sent him back with an attempted frame-up of Mac Maharaj. Yet another of the Barnard files disclosed the operation of a brothel for the sole purpose of photographing people in compromising situations. Barnard also recorded his "support network" of "prostitutes, homosexuals, nightclub owners and criminal elements".

Then Heslinga did something I consider a betrayal of Goldstone and of the trust placed in him, both as a policeman and as an official of an important body charged with uncovering the truth about matters directly related to the national interest. According to De Wet Potgieter, whose version of events is clearly based on an interview with Heslinga, the detective made a "deal" with Tolletjie Botha, giving him back the keys to ARAC's vault and saying: "Do whatever you want. I'll pick them up from you tomorrow morning."

That very night, the DCC operators gathered all the unit's incriminating documents and burnt them, throwing the ashes down an unused borehole on a smallholding outside Pretoria. The next morning, Botha returned the keys to Heslinga.

Ferdi Barnard could not possibly have been DCC's only dirty trickster. Who were the others? What did they do? How many unsolved dirty secrets of our past did Heslinga's irresponsible behaviour ensure would remain covered up?

We do know that one of the forty-eight DCC agents issued with a Diners Club credit card by the unit was Leon Flores. He was a former Vlakplaas operator who travelled to Northern Ireland in April 1992 with Captain Pamela du Randt, also of Military Intelligence, to make contact with Ulster paramilitaries. They wanted the Irish to monitor and eventually assassinate police whistle-blower Dirk Coetzee in London. Coetzee, a former commander of the Vlakplaas hit squad, had revealed the unit's existence and activities to *Vrye Weekblad* in 1989.

Flores and Du Randt were arrested by British intelligence and eventually deported to South Africa. The British government told its South African counterpart in a confidential memorandum: "Flores and Du Randt's involvement with Irish terrorist groups and their planning of a murder to take place on the streets of London is not an issue which Her Majesty's Government can ignore. Our objective is to see the issue fully investigated to our satisfaction."

We also learnt, in time, that Ferdi Barnard's long-time friend and fellow policeman, Eugene Riley, was on the DCC payroll. Riley was a murderer, a gun-runner, a brothel manager and a diamond smuggler and ran an armed robbery syndicate.

Riley's lover, Julie Wilken, told Jacques Pauw (in his book *Into the Heart of Darkness*) that Riley stole machine-guns from the SAP's Internal Stability Unit that were used in armed robberies. She also said he and Barnard beat a former criminal accomplice, Mark Francis, to death with a baseball bat in Hillbrow in August 1991.

In January 1994, Riley had Wilken type several secret documents relating to his work with DCC. Riley told her that he had turned against Barnard and expected to be killed by him. Riley was shot in his home later that month and died soon afterwards. According to Pauw, all the evidence pointed to murder.

Wilken believes that Barnard killed her boyfriend. Barnard's lover at the time, Amor Badenhorst, said he had discovered Riley's betrayal two days before the latter's death. "Ferdi was furious," she said.

Eugene Riley's death was never the subject of an inquest, but the police declared that he had committed suicide.

These were the kind of people who worked for Military Intelligence, and these were the kind of people protected by Heslinga when he facilitated the destruction of DCC's documents.

Five days after the raid on DCC, Goldstone called a press conference and issued a lengthy statement to a large number of South African and international journalists.

Minutes before Goldstone began briefing the media in Pretoria, FW de Klerk was preparing to board an aircraft home from London's Heathrow Airport, after attending a rugby test with British premier John Major. Questioned by a journalist at the airport, De Klerk said he was satisfied that the South African security forces were not involved in Third Force activities.

These words had hardly been uttered when the head of a major commission of inquiry that De Klerk himself had appointed to establish whether there was indeed such a thing as a Third Force, and whether the security forces were involved in it, confirmed what some had long since averred.

"The details I furnished at the press conference received wide publicity in South Africa and abroad and confirmed what had, for many months, been alleged by the ANC and a number of investigative journalists," says Goldstone.

It was one of the most embarrassing moments of De Klerk's political career.

Goldstone noted in his statement that Ferdi Barnard, a former police sergeant at Brixton police station, had served six years of a twenty-year jail sentence for two murders, one attempted murder and three charges of theft. On his release he was employed by the CCB. In 1991 he was recruited to the DCC by no one less than General Badenhorst, the SADF's Chief of Staff Intelligence.

"I find it morally unacceptable that a man of Barnard's past and reputation should have been employed by Military Intelligence in any capacity at all," Goldstone writes in his book.

During the last week of November 1992, João Cuna was brought before a committee of the Goldstone Commission under the chairmanship of Advocate RM Wise to give formal testimony.

Most of the people in the room were lawyers – for the SADF, for DCC, for Ferdi Barnard, for Eugene Riley and for the John Vorster Square policemen who questioned Cuna just after he turned up on *Vrye Weekblad*'s doorstep. Pearlie Joubert was there to recount her role in the saga and I was there to monitor developments, accompanied by our lawyers, Azhar Cachalia and Norman Manoim.

Cuna told the committee that Riley was the man who took him to Durban on the killing spree. Riley was a friend of Boy Schultz, the policeman at whose home he was staying at the time, he said. He confirmed that the information he had given *Vrye Weekblad* about the massacre was the truth.

The committee was sitting in a fairly small room, as far as I can remember. Riley was seated across the room from Cuna, probably about ten metres or so away. At one point during his testimony, Cuna looked in Riley's direction. I followed his gaze, as did Pearlie, she told me later. We both saw Riley looking straight at Cuna, then sliding a finger across his throat.

Cuna almost collapsed. He suddenly found it difficult to remember things, then refused to answer questions, shaking and looking down at the table in front of him.

Torie Pretorius, who led the evidence, did get it out of Cuna that

Momentum Mews, the building he had shown to Frank Dutton and Pearlie, was the one to which Barnard and Riley had taken him before their trip to Durban.

After that, Cuna refused to respond to questions. "Are you scared? Are you worried? Are you scared of someone in this room?" Pretorius asked him such pointed questions several times, but Cuna didn't respond. He understood that Riley's little gesture meant he would be killed if he spilled any more beans.

Wise adjourned the session to consult with Cuna. After a while, he returned and told the committee that Cuna was "extremely afraid" that something was going to happen to him and refused to testify any further. Any more information from Cuna would be obtained *in camera.*

That was the last we saw of João Alberto Cuna. But it wasn't the end of the drama.

After Judge Goldstone's media conference, President De Klerk came under severe pressure to take decisive measures to rein in the wild elements of his security forces. He appointed an air force general who was Deputy Chief of Operations at the time, Lieutenant General Pierre Steyn, to investigate the SADF's intelligence operations and propose a restructuring of these structures.

Steyn told me later in an interview that when he realised he didn't have enough time for a conventional inquiry, he went back to De Klerk, who then instructed National Intelligence to assist by making senior agents and researchers available. Steyn was also assisted by the SADF's Directorate Counter-Intelligence.

On 18 December 1992, De Klerk wanted a progress report, and Steyn and a senior NI man, Dr Kobus Scholtz, gave him and his senior ministers a briefing, based on material prepared by National Intelligence and the Directorate Counter-Intelligence regarding Third Force activities, the killings on trains, arming of the Inkatha Freedom Party, dirty tricks campaigns and general destabilisation of the political process.

De Klerk says in his autobiography that he was "deeply shocked" at what looked like a "rat's nest of unauthorised and illegal activities" by Military Intelligence. He now faced what he himself called "one of the most critical decisions of my presidency".

On the one hand, he dared not alienate the top structure of the SADF, already uncomfortable with his reforms and negotiations with the ANC, because this could create a climate in which a military coup became a possibility. Having a strong and loyal military behind him was one of the strongest cards De Klerk could play in the tough negotiations with the ANC.

On the other hand, it was clear that senior military elements were out of control. "It was a question of gross incompetence, or outrageous insubordination or active undermining of the state," he wrote in *The Last Trek: A New Beginning*. He had to act, or he would not only lose the significant international support he still enjoyed, but the ANC negotiators would also treat him with disrespect.

De Klerk said he even considered firing the head of the SADF, General Kat Liebenberg. He also summoned Magnus Malan, the former minister of defence under whom this rat's nest had developed, and suggested it would be a good idea for him to resign. Malan refused to do so – though he did, indeed, quit his post three months later – and warned De Klerk not to take action against senior military officers, saying he believed they were all honourable men.

De Klerk summoned the incumbent defence minister, Gene Louw, General Liebenberg, the Chief of the Army, General Georg Meiring and the head of Military Intelligence, Lieutenant General Joffel van der Westhuizen, to his office at Tuynhuys in Cape Town. Steyn was also present.

De Klerk told Liebenberg to draw up a list of officers who might be guilty of the offences described by Pierre Steyn and to propose what action should be taken against them. The three top SADF generals agreed and compiled a list of officers who had to be sacked and others whose services would be terminated due to restructuring of the intelligence services.

The next day, De Klerk announced at a sensational press conference that sixteen SADF officers, including two generals and four brigadiers, would be forced to take early retirement, while seven others would be placed on compulsory leave while investigations continued.

It was a bold step, and it put a stop to all or most of the SADF's illegal and clandestine operations, while sending strong signals to the SAP to keep their noses clean. But it also resulted in the SADF closing ranks, and all further investigations came up against a solid brick wall.

Consequently, the majority of allegations against the SADF were never really tested. As General Steyn told me: "I certainly couldn't establish without a reasonable doubt whether those allegations were true or not. All I had was the allegations and the names of people said to have been involved in these operations. The material they supplied was certainly not tested in any court of law."

Steyn expressed his unhappiness about the fact that De Klerk never made it clear that the information he gave the cabinet came from NI and the Directorate Counter-Intelligence, and that he created the impression that the list of names of "undesirable" senior officers came from Steyn himself.

"I never drew up a list and I can say that categorically," Steyn said. "The list was compiled by General Kat Liebenberg, General Georg Meiring and General Joffel van der Westhuizen, on the strict instructions of the president that he wanted names of those who should have assumed responsibility for those operations, or for preventing them." Nevertheless, Steyn was the one ostracised by the military establishment and it was his family that found itself isolated by the community.

One of the generals who was forced to quit was Chris Thirion, a bright, dynamic and popular professional soldier who was Deputy Chief of Staff Intelligence at the time.

Thirion told me in an interview that on the night the decision to make an example of some officers was made, now widely known

as the Night of the Generals, De Klerk declared: "I don't want to fire captains and majors, I want to fire generals – and I have names here of people that should be fired." Thirion's name was at the top of that list.

Thirion says he never knew about the DCC's Third Force activities and certainly never had a problem with the government's negotiations with the ANC in the interest of a political settlement. But he was something of a maverick and not liked by his superiors, which could explain why he was put on the list. When De Klerk repeated the untested allegations against him, Thirion threatened to sue him and De Klerk eventually settled out of court, stating that Thirion was never guilty of any conduct unbecoming.

Thirion told me: "I had enemies within my own family, and the long knives were out that night. I got burnt by the sun of the revolution."

It was a bad day for Chris Thirion and perhaps a few others who took a bullet for rogues, but, in hindsight, it was a very good day for South Africa and for the progress of the negotiations that brought the country freedom and democracy sixteen months later.

And it all started on that spring morning when a strange man from Mozambique presented himself at *Vrye Weekblad*'s offices in Newtown.

16

The Man with Many Names

NEWSPAPERS SIMPLY CALL IT THE ARMS DEAL SCANDAL – the large-scale corruption surrounding the South African National Defence Force's purchase of submarines, corvettes, helicopters and fighter jets for R43 billion (the figure has meanwhile ballooned to more than R50 billion). It has destroyed or tarnished several political careers and landed two top players in jail, and, by the time of writing, this drama was far from over.

But what has ended is the life of the man who started it all: the remarkable intelligence operative, spook supreme and formidable double agent known as Bheki Jacobs, who died on 9 September 2008.

He was unquestionably a secret agent of some note, but he was probably also a very moral man and a true South African patriot. At his funeral in Cape Town, the doyen of South African investigative journalism, *noseweek* editor Martin Welz, said Jacobs was a brave man of rare integrity right up to his death – and Welz doesn't readily say that kind of thing.

There were many rumours of kickbacks and underhand deals when the government signed the arms procurement deal, but the whispers remained innuendo until Patricia de Lille, then an MP for the Pan Africanist Congress, rose to her feet in parliament one sunny afternoon in September 1999 and dropped a bombshell that was to dominate the South African political scene for many years to come. She proposed a motion calling for a commission of inquiry and

named senior ANC officials who had received money in exchange for influencing the tendering process.

De Lille's information came from Bheki Jacobs. So, too, did the dossier she then sent to Judge Willem Heath's corruption-busting Special Investigative Unit.

Jacobs was born Hassan Solomon on 9 June 1962 in Cape Town, the son of Mustapha and Rookaya Solomon, née Osman. Shortly before he went to school, Hassan's mother, a member of an Indian family in Durban, decided to register her children by her maiden name because she believed that Indian schools offered better education than those for coloured children of apartheid. Mustapha Solomon was classified "Cape Malay".

Hassan Solomon thus became Hassan Osman. It was while attending Sastri College in Durban that he became politicised and fired up against the cruelties and injustices of the apartheid system. By 1982, even before he left school, he was in contact with underground operators of the African National Congress. On completion of his education, he decided to revert back to his father's name and became Hassan Solomon once again. This did not last long.

Despite being from a Muslim family, Hassan joined a youth programme run by the Diakonia Ecumenical Centre in Durban. But this was just a front that allowed him to run messages – and perhaps other materials used in the liberation struggle – between Durban and Swaziland. He was beginning to make a name for himself as a particularly cunning underground operator.

Alvin Anthony, who was also employed by Diakonia in Durban at the time, told *noseweek* in a 2001 interview: "I worked closely with Jacobs. He was an extremely committed activist and very honest, actually. He was also extremely intelligent and had a good grasp of strategic detail."

Anthony said the security police were starting to take notice of Jacobs. "He was under a lot of pressure. If he hadn't left the country, I believe he would have been killed. Only when he left did people call to say how he had helped them with their education and so on."

In 1983, at the age of twenty-one, Hassan decided to change his name officially once again, this time to Uranin Vladimir Dzerzhinsky Joseph Solomon. He explained twenty years later that taking the names of Russian Communist Party leaders (Vladimir Ilich Lenin, Feliks Dzerzhinsky, the chief of the first Soviet Secret Police, and Joseph Stalin) was aimed at avoiding security police attention – surely the security police wouldn't believe that any ANC intelligence operator would be so stupid as to assume such an obvious name!

In November 1985, the *Sunday Times* reported that the family of "UDF leader Hassan Solomon" feared that he had been assassinated by right-wingers. He disappeared while on his way to the funeral of a prominent United Democratic Front member, Victoria Mxenge, on 11 August in King William's Town, they said.

But it was all a ruse to throw the security police off his trail. Using his legal South African passport in the name of Uranin Vladimir Dzerzhinsky Joseph Solomon, he flew to the Indian Ocean island of Mauritius. According to James Sanders in *Apartheid's Friends: The Rise and Fall of South Africa's Secret Service*, the SABC reported in January 1986 that Jacobs was living with an Indian family in Mauritius, studying and playing soccer for local teams.

A few months later he travelled to Lusaka in Zambia, headquarters of the ANC in exile. The movement's intelligence arm took all his identity documents and gave him a new identity: Bheki Jacobs. During the last years of his life, most people knew him by this name.

But why change only your name if you can also change your birth date to something sexier than 9 June 1962? According to his ANC identity card issued in Lusaka, Jacobs was born on 16 December 1961 – a date significant to the ANC because it is regarded as the date on which Umkhonto we Sizwe (MK), the guerrilla army, was established. Of course, the date also holds special significance for Afrikaner nationalists, who still revere it as the Day of the Vow, the anniversary of the Voortrekkers' triumph over Zulu king Dingane's forces at Blood River in 1838.

During his life as an intelligence operator, Jacobs used several other names apart from the three he had in 1983 – Hassan Effendi, Solomon King and King Solomon among them, as well as Becky Jacobs, because it sounds like the name of a Jewish woman. But when he returned home in November 1994, his South African identity book identified him as Uranin Solomon.

From Lusaka, Jacobs was deployed for training in the ANC's camps in Zambia and Angola. It wasn't long before he encountered a phenomenon that would dominate the last years of his life and make his a household name in South Africa: corruption and authoritarianism among senior ANC leaders. His immediate response was to expose and speak out against these practices.

For that, the ANC's security bosses locked him up in the notorious Angolan prison camp called Quatro, where numerous dissidents and suspected apartheid spies were held. Many of them were tortured, some even killed. Years afterwards, Jacobs would finger his old nemesis, fellow intelligence agent Mo Shaik, for falsely accusing him of being an apartheid agent.

Jacobs later said he was tortured by men who simply wanted to know which ANC leaders he was reporting to and who the other members of his intelligence network were. He was released from Quatro after five months – some sources say by Ivan Pillay, who would eventually become a top official in the post-apartheid Secret Service, while others believe the late military commander Chris Hani effected Bheki's release, because he feared the consequences of Jacobs telling his interrogators all he knew.

Towards the end of 1986, Jacobs was deployed in Swaziland. This tiny kingdom was important to the ANC because from there it was relatively easy to cross the border into South Africa, and it also bordered on Mozambique, where the ANC had a military presence.

But the South African government and its security forces were applying huge pressure on the Swazi king and government, who cracked down on the ANC. Jacobs was one of the agents arrested

and jailed by the Swazi police. A while later he was deported to Zambia, where the ANC had its headquarters.

Jacobs couldn't stay out of trouble. When he again encountered corruption and nepotism among the leadership, he worked and lobbied against it – according to some sources, aided this time by, among others, the young Afrikaner MK member Hein Grosskopf, son of a prominent Afrikaans newspaper editor.

During this period, Jacobs surrounded himself with other committed ANC operatives who were concerned about the dishonesty among elements in the ANC's top hierarchy. After 1994, this group grew into what *noseweek* called a "guerrilla intelligence network" under the name of Congress Consultants. For a long time, the group threw its loyalty behind the man elected deputy president of the ANC in 1994 and sworn in as president of South Africa in 1999. Thabo Mbeki was seen by Jacobs and his group as the most honest of the ANC's top leadership.

In 1990, with State President FW de Klerk's unbanning of the liberation movements and the start of negotiations for a democratic settlement in South Africa, Jacobs was sent to Moscow. Two years later, he enrolled at Moscow State University's Institute of Asian and African Studies for a master's degree under old Africa hand Professor Appollon Davidson.

Noseweek wrote that Jacobs also had an "undercover diplomatic role" in the then crumbling Soviet Union: "helping to secure 'sensitive' ANC and PAC records held there, and to facilitate the return of South African trainees who found themselves stranded at various academic and military institutions". The magazine further reported that Jacobs was "unsettled and reluctant to return to South Africa, where he feared he might be killed by enemies in the ANC".

But Bheki Jacobs did come home in November 1994 and was received by the ANC's Department of Intelligence and Security under Joe Nhlanhla. Jacobs was then deployed to the Johannesburg headquarters of the ANC's Department of International Affairs, where he worked under (and, politically, for) Thabo Mbeki.

However, Jacobs was also doing work for post-apartheid South Africa's Secret Service. In a statement to the police when he was arrested in 2003 (we'll get to that in due course), Jacobs said he was registered as a Secret Service agent under the name Hassan Osman. They paid him, paid for some of his flights and bought him communication equipment, he said.

Jacobs became a key man at both Congress Consultants – which was registered as a private company in 1995 and which produced independent intelligence on events in the country – as well as in the growing camp of Mbeki's political rivals inside the ANC, who included the likes of Cyril Ramaphosa, Jacob Zuma, Mac Maharaj, Mathews Phosa and Tokyo Sexwale.

Late in 1997, Jacobs sent Mbeki a report compiled by Congress Consultants on the role that business groups were beginning to play inside the ANC. It read, in part: "Business groupings began to determine groupings and factions within the ANC ... The effect was mainly felt at local and provincial government levels, where pro-Thabo and anti-Thabo groupings were united by their business interests first and their political loyalties second. The defections and crossing over from one grouping to the next had more to do with self-interest or fall-outs in terms of business deals. This aspect has now become central in understanding the internal dynamics of the ANC."

It was probably this understanding that led Jacobs and Congress Consultants to shift their focus to the arms deal. In 1999, both he and the group were contracted by the Africa Institute, a reputable and influential research body. He continued to furnish Mbeki's office with intelligence reports and had regular meetings with the minister in the presidency, Essop Pahad.

Sobantu Xayiya was one of Jacobs's colleagues and a fellow consultant for the Africa Institute. In an interview with *noseweek*, he explained how Congress Consultants and Jacobs, its director, operated: "The type of material passed on to the director is, in most

instances, sensitive information. Often this comes from 'comrades' occupying very senior positions both in business and government.

"Sometimes people wanted discreet action taken, so that the movement was not brought into public disrepute. It was in this light that a copy of Winnie Madikizela-Mandela's letter to Jacob Zuma [about Mbeki's alleged sexual indiscretions] was passed on to the presidency long before it was leaked to the media – so that Mbeki could 'deal with it quietly'. Sometimes information comes from junior employees [about their corrupt seniors]. Because they fear victimisation, they quietly pass the information on to us."

It seems that his interest in the arms deal corruption was responsible for cooling of the relationship between Jacobs, Mbeki and the president's men. More and more information that implicated key figures in the Mbeki camp began to surface. Among them was the former minister of defence, Joe Modise, who probably took the biggest bribes of all those involved in the deal.

Jacobs approached Terry Crawford-Browne, a retired banker who became one of the most vigorous campaigners against the weapons procurement deal, in June 1999. Crawford-Browne later told the *Mail & Guardian*: "He told me: 'We'll tell you where the real corruption is – around Joe Modise and the leadership of Umkhonto we Sizwe, who see themselves as the new financial elite in post-apartheid South Africa.' Jacobs said that he and his ANC intelligence colleagues had seen the disastrous consequences in Russia of the collapse of the Soviet Union, when communists suddenly became super-capitalists. Such a gangster society, said Jacobs, was not why he had gone into exile to fight for liberation from apartheid. Something had to be done."

Jacobs was adamant that the corruption should be exposed and the rot within government and the ruling party stopped. He carefully started preparing to share his dangerous information with the rest of South Africa through opposition politicians and selected journalists. He also fed information to people inside the armaments

industry, such as industrialist Richard Young, who was unsuccessful in his bid for a tender and became one of the prime whistle-blowers and a relentless campaigner for exposure of the corrupt deals.

It was as part of this strategy that Jacobs prepared a dossier for Patricia de Lille, who dropped her bombshell in parliament in September 1999.

In late 2000, the *Sunday Times* published a report suggesting that Essop Pahad and the ANC's chief whip, Tony Yengeni, had tried to quash efforts to establish a proper investigation into the arms deal. Amid pressure from the presidency, the newspaper printed an apology on 3 December and retracted its statements.

After the apology a *Sunday Times* reporter by the name of Ranjeni Munusamy approached Crawford-Browne. She knew that he had background information and asked him to share some of this with her so that she could prove that the earlier story, for which the newspaper had apologised, was actually true.

Crawford-Browne introduced Munusamy to Jacobs on the very clear understanding that she could never reveal the agent's identity. In hindsight, it seems likely that this was a set-up.

On 11 March 2001, Munusamy and the *Sunday Times* violated one of the most sacred principles of journalism by breaking her word and exposing her source. Under the headline "Man poses as Mbeki's secret agent", the paper painted a picture of Bheki Jacobs as a crazy character with delusions of grandeur who had misrepresented himself and misled the presidency with bogus intelligence reports.

The newspaper's source was Essop Pahad himself. The editor, Mondli Makhanya, explained that he had decided to flout all journalistic principles and run the story because Jacobs "didn't play open cards with us" and because they had been told about the manner in which he had interacted with members of the presidency and spread false documents around. "Person after person in the presidency was duped by Jacobs," said Makhanya.

It wasn't Pahad and Mbeki who were duped, remarked *noseweek* in its April 2001 edition: "It is undoubtedly the *Sunday Times* that has been duped. In the spy world, Bheki Jacobs is the real deal – an experienced operative who has, for two decades, worked for the ANC at the highest levels – latterly, even for the presidency. And Pahad has foolishly committed the cardinal sin of the intelligence community – that of exposing the identity of its operatives. The *Sunday Times* appears keen to ignore the fact that what Pahad has exposed, amounts to a private Presidential intelligence network – a matter of considerable political and constitutional moment. Pahad's attempt to portray Jacobs as some kind of Walter Mitty character does not stand up to even the most cursory scrutiny."

Whatever his enemies said about Jacobs, his revelations continued to reverberate across the political landscape. In March 2001, it was revealed that Tony Yengeni had received a massive discount on his luxury four-wheel drive vehicle from DaimlerChrysler Aerospace, the recipient of one of the arms deal contracts. Yengeni had also lied about the vehicle to parliament. He eventually received a four-year jail sentence.

In August 2001 Andrew Feinstein, a senior ANC MP and a member of parliament's Standing Committee on Public Accounts (SCOPA), resigned in disgust over the way the government and the ANC had handled the controversial arms deal and the probe into alleged bribes. Feinstein later published a damning book about the corruption surrounding the deal. A few months later, Gavin Woods, the head of SCOPA, also resigned because of government's unwillingness to tolerate any real investigation into the arms deal.

The dominoes continued to tumble. In 2002, the government's arms acquisition chief, Chippy Shaik, resigned after being found in possession of classified government documents. Then his brother, Schabir, was arrested for offering a bribe of R500 000 a year to the then deputy president, Jacob Zuma. Shaik was eventually sentenced to fifteen years in jail. Zuma was also charged, but after years of delays, and just four days after Bheki Jacobs died, a High Court judge found that the prosecution of Zuma had been subject to political interference and was therefore invalid.

The smouldering power struggle between Thabo Mbeki and Jacob Zuma had burst into the open in 2003. Bulelani Ngcuka, head of the National Prosecuting Authority at the time, addressed a confidential meeting of black newspaper editors and told them that there was a "prima facie case" of corruption against Zuma, but that it wasn't "winnable" and would thus not be pursued. The editor of *City Press*, Vusi Mona, as inexperienced and gullible as his colleague at the *Sunday Times*, was the next newspaperman to break the sacred journalistic code of protecting sources, by publishing Ngcuka's off-the-record remarks. The Zuma camp retaliated by labelling Ngcuka an "apartheid spy" – an accusation that led to the president appointing the Hefer Commission of Inquiry. Among the accusers were Mo Shaik and Mac Maharaj. Mr Justice Hefer eventually found that Ngcuka was not an agent for the apartheid government.

There had long been bad blood between Mo Shaik and Bheki Jacobs, and it now resurfaced. It turned out that the group allied to Diakonia's Youth Forum in Durban in the 1980s was opposed by a group associated with the Natal Indian Congress – the "Indian Cabal", as Jacobs called them – of which the Shaiks were prominent members. Jacobs told Christelle Terreblanche, a reporter for the Independent Group: "I know too much about what Mo did in the 1980s." He said Mo Shaik was responsible for his detention in Quatro and went around telling people that Jacobs was "going to rot" in jail. When Jacobs returned home in 1994, Shaik spread the story that he was a KGB spy.

What followed was the most bizarre part of the Bheki Jacobs saga.

A document signed by the "Concerned Patriotic Intelligence Community loyal to the Constitution of the Republic of South Africa"

surfaced. It declared that a "silent coup" was being planned in South Africa by prominent figures such as then serving or former cabinet ministers Mac Maharaj, Lindiwe Sisulu and Charles Nqakula, Deputy President Jacob Zuma, police commissioner Jackie Selebi, presidential intelligence chief Billy Masethla, National Intelligence boss Vusi Mavimbela and crime intelligence chief Raymond Lalla. The document also alleged that Mo Shaik was a double agent and that his men had killed two agents in order to protect his secret. Two wealthy businessmen, Brett Kebble and Nico Shefer, were said to be bankrolling the plot.

However wild the claims sounded back in 2003, the stated aims of the coup plotters sounded very real indeed by 2008: to undermine and destroy institutions such as the Scorpions (achieved); to divide the ANC and develop offshoots of leadership (achieved); to foment conflict between Zulu- and Xhosa-speakers (partly achieved); to undermine, replace and even assassinate Thabo Mbeki (partly achieved); to determine who his successor should be (achieved); and to make South Africa ungovernable (an ongoing threat following the National Prosecuting Authority's decision to appeal against Judge Chris Nicholson's ruling that prosecution of Zuma for corruption, racketeering and money-laundering was invalid due to "political" influence).

The 2003 document also stated that there were plans to arrest Bheki Jacobs and have him killed by convicts in prison or in a staged hijacking.

Mo Shaik sent the document to Raymond Lalla, an old ANC intelligence associate and one of those named in regard to the coup plot, requesting that Jacobs be arrested. On 22 November 2003, Jacobs was picked up at his home in Cape Town, bundled into an executive jet and flown to Pretoria. His home, office and a hotel room in Pretoria where he had stayed were raided. He wasn't charged with compiling a false document, but with the very offence of which he had accused the other camp: conspiring to kill the president!

According to James Sanders, Jacobs was initially detained in the same cell as the right-wing extremists known as the Boeremag, then with a bunch of common criminals and eventually in solitary confinement.

On 28 November 2003, Sam Sole and Stefaans Brummer, two investigative journalists with the *Mail & Guardian* who had reported extensively on the arms scandal and knew Jacobs well, wrote: "Charging Jacobs, the man who had allegedly authored the warning that Mbeki was in danger of an assassination plot, with that selfsame plot, smacks of an Orwellian twist of logic."

After five days in jail, Bheki Jacobs was charged with possessing multiple passports in different names and released on bail. The charges of conspiracy to murder were dropped. After his release he said in a statement: "I deny that I am implicated in any conspiracy to murder the State President. I have devoted my entire life to the struggle for democracy in South Africa. I would never be involved in any conspiracy against a government to which I have devoted my whole life. I would go out of my way to protect the life of the State President."

Jacobs told reporters that he had informed the authorities two years earlier that he had a second passport, in the name of Hassan Osman, which he needed for an official intelligence gathering trip to North Africa.

On 16 January 2004, Economists Allied for Arms Reduction, of which former banker Terry Crawford-Browne was the South African head, declared in a statement: "The unconstitutional detention of Bheki Jacobs on 22 November 2003 on allegations that he was conspiring to murder President Thabo Mbeki is reminiscent of the jack-boot behaviour of the security forces during the apartheid era. The plot allegations have already been discredited and ridiculed. After heavily-armed police 'trashed' both his parents' and his home, Jacobs was driven to Ysterplaat air force base and flown to Pretoria in a Beechjet which is owned by the South African Police Service

and held at the disposal of Police Commissioner Jackie Selebi." The manner of his detention and the bizarre allegations of conspiracy to murder the president confirmed "gross abuse of power by the police and those persons who seemingly have influence within police circles," the statement added.

All charges against Jacobs were eventually dropped. He was diagnosed with cancer and his health deteriorated quickly before his death on 9 September 2008.

With the exception of former Western Cape premier Ebrahim Rasool, who arrived during the last minutes, there were no senior ANC leaders at his funeral in a mosque in Athlone, Cape Town. The funeral was attended by many of Bheki's friends and family members, as well as journalists Martin Welz and Stefaans Brummer and the leader of the Independent Democrats, Patricia de Lille.

Another investigative reporter from the *Mail & Guardian* who knew Jacobs well, Nic Dawes, wrote in an obituary that Jacobs was "one of the first to grasp how the headlong plunge into business would corrupt the ANC, how its internal politics would become a savage contest for resources, and just how early in its victory the party would lose its way."

Dawes concluded: "He is gone, but the South Africa he saw emerging behind the bright platitudes of the 1990s is now manifest all around us. Being right was no comfort to him."

South African History at a Glance

100 000+ years ago:	Modern human beings, *Homo sapiens*, develop on African soil from the Cape to Ethiopia.
6 000+ years ago:	Nomadic herders of sheep and cattle called the Khoikhoi, who had developed in the northern regions of today's Botswana, move south into South Africa. There they join their close relatives, the aboriginal hunters called the San or Bushmen.
1 000 years ago:	Bantu-speaking farmers, who had gradually migrated south from the Great Lakes region over more than a millennium, form a rich, powerful kingdom at Mapungubwe in northern South Africa. Over the next 500 years, different groups move down the east coast and central areas of South Africa.
1488:	The Portuguese seafarer Bartholomew Dias becomes the first European to set foot on South African soil when he lands at Mossel Bay. His party is met by Khoikhoi. Eleven years later, Dias's colleague Vasco da Gama goes ashore at the same spot and plants a *padrão* (a large stone cross inscribed with Portugal's coat of arms). As Da Gama's ships sail away, those on board see the Khoikhoi defiantly push the *padrão* over.
1510:	Portugal's viscount Francisco d'Almeida anchors his ships in what will become Table Bay. He and his men go ashore and get into a fight with the Khoikhoi. The viscount and fifty of his men are killed.
1652:	A representative of the Dutch East India Company, Jan van Riebeeck, establishes a refreshment station at the Cape. It is the first permanent

settlement of Europeans in South Africa. Van Riebeeck plants a hedge of bitter almond on the outskirts of the settlement to keep settlers and Khoikhoi apart – the first act of apartheid.

1657: The Dutch take Khoikhoi leader Doman to Batavia. On his return he becomes the first Khoikhoi freedom fighter, leading attacks against the Dutch settlers.

1658: The first ships carrying slaves arrive at the Cape. The slaves come from Dahomey, Angola, Mozambique and Madagascar, and in larger numbers from India and the East Indies. In total, some 60 000 slaves are brought to the Cape.

1671: Sara, a Khoikhoi woman who tried to integrate into Dutch colonial society, commits suicide in the sheep shed of freed slave Angela van Bengalen. As far as is known, Sara was the first Khoi person to commit suicide.

1688: The first French Huguenots arrive at the Cape. The Dutch, French and later German arrivals form a new group (infused from time to time with slave and Khoikhoi blood) that later becomes known as the Afrikaners.

1713: Large numbers of Khoikhoi die during a smallpox epidemic.

1786: Two great South Africans are born: Moshoeshoe, the founder and king of the Basotho, and Shaka, founder and king of the Zulu.

1795: Britain conquers the Cape Colony, gives it back to the Dutch in 1803, but recaptures it in 1806.

1819: The Xhosa mystic and war-doctor Makhanda leads a force of 10 000 men in an unsuccessful attack on the British garrison at Grahamstown.

1820: The British settle some four thousand British subjects, mostly farmers and tradesmen, in the Eastern Cape. Makhanda escapes from Robben Island but drowns when his boat capsizes near Bloubergstrand.

1822: The Batlokoa of the chieftainess Mantatisi are attacked by the amaHlubi. This signals the beginning of a great social and military upheaval called the Lifaqane.

1828: Shaka is assassinated by his half-brothers Dingane and Mhlangana.

1834: Xhosa king Hintsa is killed during a savage war with the British colonial forces. In 1850, some 16 000 Xhosa are killed in another war.

1836: The Afrikaner trekboers in the Eastern Cape start their migration into the interior, later called the Great Trek, eventually clashing with black chiefdoms north of the Gariep River.

1838: The Voortrekkers defeat a Zulu force at the Battle of Blood River.

1843: Britain annexes Natal, ending the independence of the Voortrekker Republic of Natalia. The Boers declare the South African Republic (Zuid-Afrikaansche Republiek, or ZAR), with Pretoria as capital.

1854: The Boer republic of the Orange Free State is proclaimed and conflict with the Basotho begins. Whites have now settled in most parts of South Africa.

1860: The first shiploads of indentured labourers from India arrive in Natal to work on the sugar plantations.

1873: A number of Boer families set out on a journey to present-day Namibia and Angola – the start of the Dorsland Trek.

1876: Diamonds are discovered at Kimberley.

1886: Gold is discovered at present-day Johannesburg.

1893: Mohandas Gandhi arrives from India and inspires and organises resistance against discriminatory practices.

1896: Leander Starr Jameson leads a disastrous invasion of Johannesburg on behalf of Cecil John Rhodes and his "uitlander" supporters.

1899: The ZAR declares war against Britain and is joined by the Orange Free State.

1902: The two Boer republics surrender and sign the Peace of Vereeniging. Almost 30 000 Boer women and children, and a similar number of black people, died during the war.

1910: The Union of South Africa, consisting of the two Boer republics and the two British colonies, comes into being. Black people are denied the vote.

1912: The South African Native National Congress is formed in Bloemfontein to campaign for black rights. The name is later changed to the African National Congress (ANC).

1914: The National Party is formed in Bloemfontein as a primary political vehicle for Afrikaner nationalism. Boer War general Koos de la Rey is mistaken for the fleeing Foster gang and shot dead by police in Johannesburg.

1918: The secret, all-powerful Afrikaner Broederbond is formed to further the cause of Afrikaner nationalism in business, education and culture.

1938: Afrikaner nationalism experiences a major surge with the national re-enactment of the Great Trek a century earlier.

1948: The National Party wins the white general election and starts putting its ideology of apartheid into practice.

1952: The ANC gains momentum as a resistance movement with the successful Defiance Campaign to protest racial laws.

1955: Delegates from all over South Africa adopt the Freedom Charter at Kliptown. It remains a crucial policy document for almost forty years.

1957: Africanists in the ANC break away because of the Freedom Charter's non-racial clauses and form the Pan Africanist Congress (PAC), with Robert Sobukwe as founding president.

1960: Police kill sixty-nine people at a protest meeting against the pass laws in Sharpeville, and three at a march in Langa, Cape Town. The killings evoke an international outcry. The government outlaws the ANC, the PAC and the South African Communist Party (SACP). On 9 April, David Beresford Pratt shoots Prime Minister Hendrik Verwoerd in the face at the Rand Easter Show, but Verwoerd survives.

1961: South Africa is declared a republic and leaves the Commonwealth. The ANC decides to launch an armed struggle and forms a military wing known as Umkhonto we Sizwe (MK). A sabotage campaign is launched on 16 December.

1962: Nelson Mandela is arrested and sentenced to five years in prison for leaving the country illegally.

1963: Walter Sisulu, Govan Mbeki, Ahmed Kathrada and other members of MK's High Command are arrested at Lilliesleaf farm, Rivonia. The first of several black bantustans, the Transkei, becomes self-governing. The policy is that black South Africans should exercise their political rights in these "homelands", of which four later become "independent".

1964: Mandela and the Rivonia detainees are sentenced to life imprisonment under the Sabotage Act and taken to Robben Island.

1966: Prime Minister Hendrik Verwoerd is stabbed to death in parliament by a messenger, Dimitri Tsafendas. John Vorster becomes prime minister.

1967: District Six, a vibrant Cape Town suburb inhabited mostly by coloureds, is declared a "white area", as are various other residential areas. The people are forcibly removed to new and distant townships on the Cape Flats and at Mitchells Plain.

1974: Government decides to launch a programme to manufacture nuclear weapons. A coup in Portugal leads to the independence of its African colonies, Angola and Mozambique.

1975: South African forces invade Angola to fight on the side of UNITA and the FNLA. Cuban forces arrive at the same time in support of the ruling MPLA.

1976: Pupils in Soweto protest against Bantu Education and the use of Afrikaans as a language of instruction. The police kill a number of protestors, leading to a nationwide revolt in townships. Many black youngsters leave the country to join the ANC in neighbouring states.

1977: Charismatic Black Consciousness leader Steve Biko is assaulted by police, thrown naked into a police van and driven to Pretoria. He dies on the way. Justice minister Jimmy Kruger says Biko's death leaves him cold.

1978: Prime Minister John Vorster resigns after a scandal over the misuse of secret funds for the Department of Information. He is replaced by his minister of defence, PW Botha, who appoints the South African Defence Force chief, Magnus Malan, as minister of defence. The militarisation of South Africa begins and a programme of military destabilisation of neighbouring states follows.

1980: Zimbabwe becomes independent, with ZANU leader Robert Mugabe as its first president.

1983: PW Botha wins a referendum on proposals to institute separate houses of parliament for coloureds and Indians. Black South Africans remain barred from political participation. The "Tricameral Parliament" angers the majority of South Africans, leading to formation of the United Democratic Front (UDF). It is ideologically aligned with the ANC, as is one of its major constituencies, the newly formed Congress of South African Trade Unions. A period of severe repression and resistance starts, with several states of emergency being declared.

1984: South Africa and Mozambique sign the Nkomati Accord, a non-aggression treaty.

1989: PW Botha suffers a stroke and is succeeded as National Party leader by FW de Klerk. Botha meets Mandela. De Klerk takes over as state president and releases some senior ANC leaders from jail. The Berlin Wall falls. SWAPO wins a landslide victory in Namibia's independence elections.

1990: De Klerk announces the unbanning of the ANC, SACP and PAC at the opening of parliament. Mandela walks out of prison on 11 February. ANC exiles start returning home. The ANC and the NP sign the Groote Schuur Accord, committing themselves to ending political violence and negotiating a democratic settlement. Namibia becomes an independent republic.

1991: All negotiating parties sign the National Peace Accord. The political violence continues. The first meeting of the Conference for a Democratic South Africa (CODESA) takes place.

1992: A referendum among white voters gives De Klerk a strong mandate for negotiations. Forty people are massacred at Boipatong and the ANC breaks off all talks with the government. The ANC's Cyril Ramaphosa and the NP's Roelf Meyer form a "special channel of communication" and resume negotiations that lead to the signing of a Record of Understanding.

1993: On 10 April, popular ANC and SACP leader Chris Hani is assassinated by a right-winger. Former SADF chief General Constand Viljoen mobilises tens of thousands of white men countrywide for possible military intervention, and they embark on a limited sabotage campaign. The multi-party conference ratifies an interim constitution.

1994: On 27–28 April South Africa's first non-racial elections take place and the ANC wins almost two-thirds of the votes. Nelson Mandela is sworn in as the first democratic president.

1996: The final text of the Constitution of South Africa is agreed to by parliament and ratified by the Constitutional Court. The Truth and Reconciliation Commission begins its hearings.

1999: Nelson Mandela retires as president after a general election and is succeeded by Thabo Mbeki. Opposition politician Patricia de Lille accuses senior ANC leaders of accepting bribes during a lucrative arms procurement process.

2007: Amid a popular revolt in the ruling ANC, Thabo Mbeki is replaced by Jacob Zuma as president of the party during its national congress in Polokwane.

2008: The ANC leadership forces Mbeki to resign and he is replaced by the deputy president of the party, Kgalema Motlanthe.

Bibliography

Arbousset, Thomas. *Missionary Excursion.* Morija: Morija Museum and Archives, 1991.

Barbary, James. *The Boer War.* London: Victor Gollancz, 1971.

Becker, Peter. *Hill of Destiny: The Life and Times of Moshesh, Founder of the Basotho.* London: Panther, 1969.

———. *Path of Blood: The Rise and Conquest of Mzilikazi, Founder of the Matabele.* London: Granada, 1975.

Birkby, Carel. *Thirstland Treks.* London: Faber & Faber, 1936.

Casalis, Eugéne. *The Basutos.* Facsimile reprint of the 1861 edition. Morija: Morija Museum and Archives, 1997.

Coates, Austin. *Basutoland.* London: Her Majesty's Stationery Office, 1966.

Coetzee, J Albert. *Groot Avontuur: Sketse uit die Dorslandtrek.* Transvaal Publishing, 1976.

Collins, Robert O, and James M Burns. *A History of Sub-Saharan Africa.* Cambridge: Cambridge University Press, 2007.

Couzens, Tim. *Murder at Morija.* Johannesburg: Random House, 2003.

Davenport, Rodney, and Christopher Saunders. *South Africa: A Modern History.* London: Macmillan, 2000.

Deacon, Harriet (ed.). *The Island.* Cape Town: David Philip, 1996.

De Klerk, FW. *The Last Trek: A New Beginning.* London: Macmillan, 1999.

De Klerk, WA. *The Thirstland.* Durban: Bok Books, 1988.

Eldredge, Elizabeth. *A South African Kingdom: The Pursuit of Security in Nineteenth-Century Lesotho.* Cambridge: Cambridge University Press, 1993.

Ellenberger, David-Frédéric. *History of the Basuto, Ancient and Modern.* Facsimile reprint of 1912 edition. Morija: Morija Museum and Archives, 1997.

Elphick, Richard. *Khoikhoi and the Founding of White South Africa.* Johannesburg: Ravan Press, 1985.

Fisher, John. *Paul Kruger: His Life and Times.* London: Secker & Warburg, 1974.

Gasa, Nomboniso. *Women in South African History.* Cape Town: HSRC Press, 2006.

Germond, RC. *Chronicles of Basutoland.* Morija: Morija Sesuto Book Depot, 1967.

Giliomee, Hermann. *The Afrikaners: Biography of a People.* Cape Town: Tafelberg, 2003.

Giliomee, Hermann, and Richard Elphick (eds.). *'n Samelewing in Wording: Suid-Afrika 1652–1840.* Cape Town: Maskew Miller Longman, 1990.

——— (eds.). *The Shaping of South African Society 1652–1820.* Cape Town: Maskew Miller Longman, 1984.

Gill, Stephen J. *A Short History of Lesotho.* Morija: Morija Museum and Archives, 1993.

Goldstone, Richard J. *For Humanity: Reflections of a War Crimes Investigator.* Johannesburg: Witwatersrand University Press, 2000.

Hamann, Hilton. *Days of the Generals.* Cape Town: Zebra Press, 2001.

Jooste, JP. *Gedenkboek van die Dorslandtrek.* Potchefstroom: Herald, 1974.

Johnson, RW. *South Africa: The First Man, the Last Nation.* Johannesburg & Cape Town: Jonathan Ball, 2005.

Karsten, Chris. *Dodelike Vroue: Wanneer Passie in Bloed Eindig.* Cape Town: Human & Rousseau, 2007.

Kruger, Paul. *The Memoirs of Paul Kruger.* London: T Fisher Unwin, 1902.

Laband, John. *Rope of Sand: The Rise and Fall of the Zulu Kingdom in the Nineteenth Century.* Johannesburg & Cape Town: Jonathan Ball, 1995.

Longford, Elizabeth. *Jameson's Raid.* Johannesburg & Cape Town: Jonathan Ball, 1962.

Loos, Jackie. *Echoes of Slavery: Voices from South Africa's Past.* Cape Town: David Philip, 2004.

Ludi, Gerard, and Blaar Grobbelaar. *Die Verbasende Bram Fischer.* Cape Town: Nasionale Boekhandel, 1966.

Malan, Magnus. *My Life with the SA Defence Force.* Pretoria: Protea Book House, 2006.

Mandela, Nelson. *Long Walk to Freedom: The Autobiography of Nelson Mandela.* Randburg: Macdonald Purnell, 1994.

May, Henry John, and Ian Hamilton. *Die Dood van Generaal de la Rey.* Cape Town: Nasionale Boekhandel, n.d.

Meintjes, Johannes. *The Voortrekkers.* London: Corgi Books, 1975.

Mitchell, Peter. *The Archaeology of Southern Africa.* Cambridge: Cambridge University Press, 2002.

Morris, Donald R. *The Washing of the Spears.* London: Cardinal, 1973.

Mostert, Noël. *Frontiers: The Epic of South Africa's Creation and the Tragedy of the Xhosa People.* London: Jonathan Cape, 1992.

Muller, CFJ (ed.). *500 Years: A History of South Africa.* Pretoria: Academica, 1975.

Naidoo, Jay. *History in Africa,* vol. 12, pp. 187–210. African Studies Association, 1985.

O'Malley, Padraig. *Shades of Difference: Mac Maharaj and the Struggle for South Africa.* New York: Viking, 2007.

Pakenham, Thomas. *The Boer War.* London: Abacus, 1991.

Pauw, Jacques. *Into the Heart of Darkness.* Johannesburg & Cape Town: Jonathan Ball, 1997.

Peires, Jeff. *The House of Phalo: A History of the Xhosa People in the Days of their Independence.* Johannesburg & Cape Town: Jonathan Ball, 2003.

Penn, Nigel. *Rogues, Rebels and Runaways: Eighteenth-Century Cape Characters.* Cape Town: David Philip, 1999.

———. *The Forgotten Frontier: Colonist and Khoisan on the Cape's Northern Frontier in the 18th Century.* Cape Town: Double Storey, 2005.

Potgieter, De Wet. *Total Onslaught: Apartheid's Dirty Tricks Exposed.* Cape Town: Zebra Press, 2007.

Ritter, EA. *Shaka Zulu: The Rise of the Zulu Empire.* London: Longmans Green & Co., 1955.

Rhoodie, Denys. *Conspirators in Conflict: A Study of the Johannesburg Reform Committee and its Role in the Conspiracy against the South African Republic.* Cape Town: Tafelberg, 1967.

Ross, Robert. *A Concise History of South Africa.* Cambridge: Cambridge University Press, 1999.

Rotberg, Robert I. *The Founder: Cecil Rhodes and the Pursuit of Power.* Johannesburg & Cape Town: Jonathan Ball, 2002.

Schoeman, Karel. *Early Slavery at the Cape of Good Hope 1652–1717.* Pretoria: Protea Book House, 2007.

———. *Kinders van die Kompanjie: Kaapse Lewens uit die Sewentiende Eeu.* Pretoria: Protea Book House, 2006.

Sweetman, David. *Women Leaders in African History.* London: Heinemann Educational Books, 1984.

Van Tonder, JM. *Kerk in 'n Beter Land: Die Kerkverhaal van die Dorsland- en Angola Trekkers 1873–1937.* n.d.

Van Woerden, Henk. *A Mouthful of Glass.* Johannesburg & Cape Town: Jonathan Ball, 2000.

Wannenburgh, Alf. *Forgotten Frontiersmen.* Cape Town: Howard Timmins, 1978.

Wells, Julia C. *Rebellion and Uproar: Makhanda and the Great Escape from Robben Island, 1820.* Pretoria: University of South Africa Press, 2007.

Glossary

braai:	barbecue
broedertwis:	quarrel between brothers
dominee:	reverend
goeie Boeremeisie:	good Afrikaner girl
karos:	cloak made of animal skin
kraal:	animal enclosure or traditional rural settlement of huts and houses
laager:	circle of ox wagons forming defensive barricade
uitlander:	foreigner
veldkornet:	field-cornet
veldwagtmeester:	field guard
VOC:	Dutch East India Company (Vereenigde Oost-Indische Compagnie)
Volksraad:	People's Assembly

Index

Do you have any comments, suggestions or
feedback about this book or any other Zebra Press titles?
Contact us at **talkback@zebrapress.co.za**